As one of the world's longest established
and best-known travel brands,
Thomas Cook are the experts in trave

For more than 135 years c
guidebooks have unlocked the secr
of destinations around the wo
sharing with travellers a wealth
experience and a passion for travel.

**Rely on Thomas Cook as your
travelling companion on your next trip
and benefit from our unique heritage.**

Thomas Cook **traveller** guides

MOSCOW &
ST PETERSBURG
Chris Booth

ion since 1873

Written by Chris Booth, updated by Marc Di Duca
Original photography by Demetrio Carrasco, Ken Paterson and Jon Arnold,
updated photography by Marc Di Duca

Published by Thomas Cook Publishing
A division of Thomas Cook Tour Operations Limited.
Company Registration No 3772199 England
The Thomas Cook Business Park, Unit 9, Coningsby Road,
Peterborough PE3 8SB, United Kingdom
Email: books@thomascook.com, Tel: + 44 (0) 1733 416477
www.thomascookpublishing.com

Produced by Cambridge Publishing Management Limited
Burr Elm Court, Main Street, Caldecote CB23 7NU

ISBN: 978-1-84848-221-0

© 2004, 2006, 2008 Thomas Cook Publishing
This fourth edition © 2010
Text © Thomas Cook Publishing
Maps © Thomas Cook Publishing/PCGraphics (UK) Limited
Transport maps © Communicarta Limited

Series Editor: Maisie Fitzpatrick
Production/DTP: Steven Collins

Printed and bound in Italy by Printer Trento

Cover photography: © Giovanni Simeone/4CR

Contents

Introduction

Russia – few do not feel at least a tinge of excitement at the mere mention of the word. It conjures up images of sleigh rides through snow-bound natural beauty and Chekhovian civility, bloody revolution and inspired arts, bleak communist uniformity and mafia hitmen. Churchill's 'riddle wrapped in a mystery inside an enigma' is as baffling and diverse as ever, but also open for visitors to discover it like never before.

The Russians' depths and paradoxes cannot be better revealed to the foreign visitor than through the two great cities of Moscow (Moskva) and St Petersburg (Sankt Peterburg), the former the current and one-time capital of the nation, the latter having spent a brief two centuries in the role. Today they both glitter under the gilt onion spires of newly renovated churches; blossoming arts and cultural scenes fill the streets with colourful festivals and pulsating nightlife keeps the beat going until the small hours.

But things were not always so. In the 1980s both cities were brought to their knees by crumbling communist inefficiencies and Mikhail Gorbachev's twin policies of *perestroika* (restructuring) and *glasnost* (openness), which plunged the nation into economic disarray. Both cities emerged bloody but unbowed from the turbulent 1990s when the country's own leaders pummelled the parliament with tank fire, and mafia killings were as frequent as the traffic accidents which littered both cities' potholed

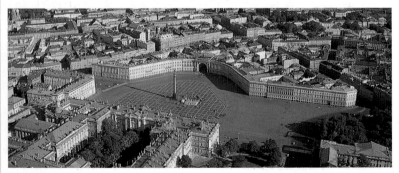

Palace Square, St Petersburg

The former might of the Soviet Union is represented by statues like this across the Russian Federation

Russian Federation

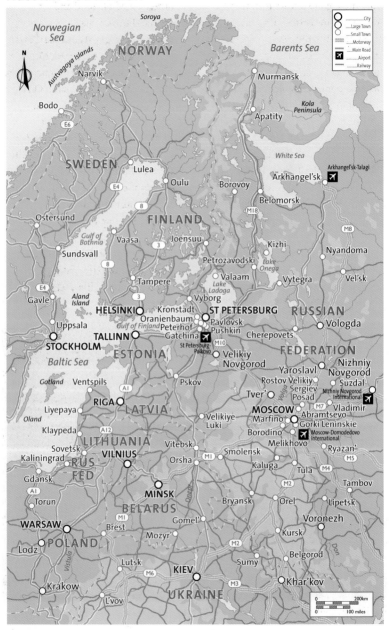

roads. Much of the credit for the new order must go to once-and-future President (now prime minister) Vladimir Putin. But while his economic and social successes at home have made this less-than-charismatic leader one of the most popular residents of the Kremlin in the nation's history, he has, in Western eyes, returned a tinge of despotism to this vast land.

'If ever your sons should be discontented with France, try my recipe', wrote the Marquis de Custine after a visit to Russia in the 19th century. 'Tell them to go to Russia. It is a useful journey for every foreigner: who has examined the country will be content to live anywhere else.' The sentiment was echoed for another hundred years and in travellers' tales of morose shopkeepers, police informers, inedible food and belligerent bureaucrats.

Though these ghosts of Russia's past have yet to be fully exorcised, Moscow and St Petersburg today are much more palatable to the foreign visitor. On a visit to this Slavic double-act you should embrace the post-Soviet disarray, revel in the Russian people's warmth and overwhelming hospitality which lurk beneath stony expressions, breathe in the billowing incense of its churches where you can witness religion in the raw, and wander the halls of its unsurpassed museums and galleries in awe. Whatever the labyrinthine mysteries of this fascinating country, it is certain never to disappoint.

The colourful domes of St Basil's Cathedral, Moscow

The land

Situated close to Russia's western frontier, St Petersburg was once the hub of a vast empire reaching 9,500km (5,900 miles) eastwards from the Baltic coast to the Pacific Ocean and almost 5,000km (3,105 miles) from the Arctic to the Caspian Sea. Today the successor to that empire, the Russian Federation, still extends over a staggering nine time zones of Russian territory. Its capital is Moscow.

The basics

Built on the important Moskva River, Moscow was ideally placed to dominate trade among the Russian princedoms. It never looked back. With a population of almost ten million, Moscow is today the world's sixth-largest city and the focus of the aspirations of most of Russia's other 143 million citizens.

St Petersburg is the most northerly of the world's big cities and its five million inhabitants share the same latitude with those of Anchorage in Alaska. Its 44 islands are in the Neva delta on the Gulf of Finland, making for a damp and windy climate. Summer evenings are long, especially the White Nights from 25 May to 16 July. The longest 'day' (around 21 June) actually lasts for 18,453 minutes!

As Hitler and Napoleon discovered, winter can be formidably cold, as low as −42°C (−44°F) in Moscow. 'Russia has two generals in which she can trust,' Nicholas I remarked, 'Generals Janvier and Février.'

While both cities churn out machine tools, vehicles and chemicals, ever more people are turning to the once despised profession of *biznismyen*, trading whatever comes their way and satisfying a nation long starved of consumer goods.

The economics of reform

Economics rather than politics spelt the end for the communist system. A series of Five Year Plans had huge success in turning the USSR into an industrial giant. But growth of six per cent a year had collapsed to negative figures by the mid-1980s. Harvests rotted in the fields and life was characterised by the saying: 'We pretend to work and they pretend to pay us.'

In the end, the October Revolution proved no match for the information revolution. Herculean tractor production figures were meaningless in a world dominated by computers: in 1987, the USSR possessed just 100,000 personal computers compared with US annual production of over five million! Something had to change.

The cost of communism

Following Stalin's declaration that 'there are no fortresses that communism cannot storm', Soviet planners in quest of ever-higher economic targets wreaked havoc with the environment. A scheme to reverse the flow of Siberia's rivers was narrowly avoided, but the country is scarred by other ecological disasters.

Pollution in some industrial cities is so high that rates of cancer and other diseases are sky high. Lake Baikal, containing a fifth of the world's drinking water, was until recently dirtied by waste from a cellulose plant on its southern shores. Parts of western Russia were severely affected by the nuclear accident at Chernobyl in Ukraine and air quality in Moscow is one of the worst in Europe. In St Petersburg, a city built on the shores of the Gulf of Finland, tap water has to be boiled before consumption.

Pollution combined with smoking, alcohol, poor diet and stress accounts for people's low life expectancy – 61 for men and 73 for women.

Mighty Russia

For all the pain of reform, Russia's natural and human wealth is unrivalled. Massive reserves of oil, coal and natural gas remain to be tapped, attracting Western investors to the Siberian permafrost, while the Ural Mountains comprise 2,000km (1,240 miles) of rich mineral deposits. Timber resources are similarly assured – well over half the country is densely forested. What's more, the population is highly educated: the USSR boasted nearly 15 million active scientists and engineers.

This vast cohort of engineers and technicians ensures that Russian technology, backed by vast resources, is slowly regaining its once lost fame. Medical breakthroughs and high-tech military and aviation improvements are regularly made public. They are not improvements merely stated on paper, as was often the case in the past, but real, tangible progress.

The Moskva River, where it passes the Kremlin

The land

History

988	Prince Vladimir, ruler of the Russian state in Kiev, converts to Christianity.
1147	Yuri Dolgorukiy (Long Arm) establishes Moscow at the confluence of the Moskva and Neglinnaya rivers. Moscow becomes capital of the Principality of Muscovy.
1237	Batu Khan of the Golden Horde sacks Moscow. Mongol domination is to last for two and a half centuries.
1453	The fall of Constantinople. Moscow henceforth is referred to as the 'Third and Last Rome'. The Byzantine double-headed eagle becomes the emblem of state.
1584	Ivan IV ('the Terrible') dies. Brutal regimentation of a poor land and people has made Muscovy a formidable European power.
1613	Mikhail Romanov is elected Tsar of all the Russias; his dynasty will last until 1917.
1682	Peter the Great's accession to the throne aged ten.
1703	Peter the Great founds St Petersburg on 16 May.
1712	Moscow razed by fire. St Petersburg is proclaimed the new capital.
1789	The French Revolution quashes Catherine the Great's experiment with liberalism.
1812	Napoleon invades Russia. Muscovites burn their city to drive out the invaders.
1825	Decembrists' revolt, led by educated officers later exiled to eastern Siberia or executed.
1854	The Crimean War lays bare the backwardness of Russian society.
1861	Alexander II's decree abolishing serfdom.
1881	Alexander II is assassinated by terrorists belonging to the revolutionary People's Will movement.
1894	Nicholas II ascends the throne.
1905	Revolutionary disturbances throughout Russia result in

the introduction of a constitution and an elected assembly (Duma).

1917 The February Revolution leads to the abdication of Nicholas II. The Provisional Government is in power until the Bolshevik putsch on 25 October. On 16 November Moscow is restored as capital.

1918 The tsar and his family are executed. Civil war and foreign intervention last until 1921.

1922 The Union of Soviet Socialist Republics is founded.

1924 Lenin's death on 24 January followed by a power struggle (from which Stalin emerges victorious). St Petersburg – which was renamed Petrograd in 1914 – becomes Leningrad.

1928 The first Five Year Plan collectivises farms, leading to famine and the death of an estimated five million.

1934 The assassination of Sergei Kirov, Leningrad's Party chief, heralds a period of purges and show trials.

1941 The Soviet Union enters World War II. Leningrad is under siege and German troops reach the outskirts of Moscow. Something approaching 27 million die during the war.

1953 Death of Stalin.

1956 Khrushchev's 'Secret Speech' to the 20th Party Congress denounces Stalin and initiates a limited and brief thaw.

1964 Khrushchev is replaced as General Secretary of the Soviet Communist Party by Leonid Brezhnev.

1979 The USSR invades Afghanistan.

1980 The Moscow Olympics are boycotted by the USA.

1985 Mikhail Gorbachev becomes Communist Party General Secretary in March and introduces the policies of *glasnost* (openness) and *perestroika* (restructuring).

1986 Andrei Sakharov, human rights campaigner, is released from internal exile.

1987 Boris Yeltsin is sacked as Moscow Party boss after openly attacking Gorbachev.

1989 First democratic elections take place. Revolutions throughout the Soviet bloc lead to the fall of the Berlin Wall.

1991 The citizens of Leningrad vote to restore the city's name to St Petersburg. After a failed communist coup, Yeltsin – now Russian president – declares the Communist Party illegal. The USSR is dissolved, and the Commonwealth of Independent States (CIS) is formed in December. Gorbachev resigns on Christmas Day.

1992 'Shock therapy' introduced, abolishing price controls overnight on 2 January. Reform is deadlocked by parliament.

1993 In September the Russian parliament rebels after Boris Yeltsin suspends the constitution. Yeltsin loyalists eventually recapture the parliament building (White House). A new constitution is adopted in December.

1994 Yeltsin orders troops into the breakaway republic of Chechnya, suffering heavy losses militarily and in the opinion polls.

1996 In July Yeltsin is re-elected. In December, the last military units leave Chechnya.

1997 Yeltsin orders government to pay salaries and pensions. This is not met and unions threaten strikes. In May peace treaty is signed between Russia and Chechnya. World Bank provides further loans.

1998 March crisis on Russia's stock markets. Rouble devalues rapidly and government is in crisis.

1999 In August, Chechen fighters make incursions into Dagestan. President Yeltsin names new prime minister – Vladimir Putin. Some see this as a tactic to avoid prosecution after he leaves office. Russian forces return to Chechnya in answer to bomb attacks in Moscow. President Yeltsin finally gives up office.

2000 Vladimir Putin is elected president of Russian Federation. Disaster strikes

Kursk nuclear submarine in Barents Sea. Britain and other NATO states offer to assist the recovery operation in a bid to save any survivors, but Russia refuses.

2001 Russia supports US action in Afghanistan in retaliation for terrorist attacks on 11 September. This helps Russia justify anti-terrorist action in Chechnya.

2002 In October Chechen terrorists take more than 800 people hostage in the Dubrovka Theatre, Moscow. The subsequent assault by special forces goes wrong and 130 hostages die from the effects of gas.

2003 Celebrations marking the 300th anniversary of St Petersburg are attended by international politicians. Chechen suicide bombers kill 13 at a suburban rock festival in Moscow.

2004 In March President Putin is returned to power, winning more than 70 per cent of the popular vote. In August two Chechen suicide bombers blow up two passenger airliners, killing everyone on board. A week later a bomb kills ten in a Moscow metro station, and the following day Chechen terrorists enter a school in Beslan, North Ossetia, taking everyone hostage. Hundreds die, many of them children, in the ensuing rescue bid.

2005 In May more than 50 state and government heads attend the celebrations marking the 60th anniversary of the end of World War II. The same month the powerful former head of Yukos Oil, Mikhail Khodorkovsky, is found guilty of fraud and tax evasion and sentenced to nine years in prison.

2007 Boris Yeltsin, Russia's first democratically elected president, dies in April aged 76.

2008 Dmitry Medvedev succeeds Putin as president; Putin becomes prime minister. World economic crisis hits Russia particularly hard. Russia fights a short war with neighbouring Georgia, souring relations with the West.

2009–14 Preparations to hold the 2014 Winter Olympics continue in Sochi.

October 1917

Glorified in countless films, novels and paintings, the 'Great October Revolution' was more akin to a vaudeville farce than the dawn of the regime that was to grip Russia for over 70 years.

Vladimir Ulyanov – 'Lenin' (1870–1924), in hiding and disguised by a badly fitting wig and glasses, desperately harangued his colleagues to start a revolution that most of

Lenin mural on the Moscow metro

them, including Stalin, were against. Despite their name, meaning 'The Majority', Lenin's Bolsheviks were few and only one of many opposition factions. Knowing that they had no hope of winning elections scheduled for November, Lenin was determined to grab power by force, and on the night of 25 October (7 November in the 'New Style' – Western – calendar), the Bolsheviks sent troops to occupy key positions in Petrograd. Not a shot was fired in anger.

Lenin penned a notice declaring the government deposed that was pasted around the city the next morning. Petrograd was unmoved: according to eyewitness accounts, offices and shops opened on time and opera-lovers looked forward to Chaliapin's evening performance at the Mariinskiy Theatre.

A haphazard siege of the Winter Palace, where the government unconcernedly sat on, was organised. Lenin emerged from hiding to make a short appearance at the Petrograd Soviet, the assembly of opposition parties, informing it that the worldwide socialist revolution had begun that night.

The 'storm' began at 9.40pm when a shot from the cruiser *Aurora*,

Revolution Arch, VDNKh, Moscow

moored downstream, broke the peace. But since the ship had just completed a refit, there were no live rounds and the revolutionaries had to make do with a blank shell.

Far from the frontal assault of grizzled workers, popularised in Sergei Eisenstein's film *October*, the first Bolshevik forces slipped into the building through open windows. The final death toll – five – resulted from stray bullets rather than spirited resistance by the Provisional Government, which was finally arrested and led away a little after 2am the following morning.

Politics

Steeped in ethnic conflict and economic chaos, the mighty Soviet Union lurched to an undignified halt on Christmas Day 1991, when Mikhail Gorbachev resigned the presidency of an extinct superpower. Nearly three-quarters of a century of communist rule was over.

The *ancien régime*

Article 6 of the Soviet Union's constitution enshrined the role of the Communist Party and its 20 million members as 'the leading and guiding force of Soviet society'. Every farm and factory had its Party cell that supervised decisions emanating from the ruling Central Committee and Politburo. The nerve centre of the system, the Politburo met every Thursday under the guidance of the Party General Secretary, the country's leader.

The Party appointed all key officials, and its élite were rewarded with special medical care, access to closed shops and imported goods, country houses and hunting reserves. They were, in the subtle Russian distinction, *lyudi* rather than *naseleniye* – 'people' rather than 'population'. Their children could look forward to easy entry into the Party, university and the choicest jobs. The system, it seemed, was self-perpetuating.

The beginning of the end

Lionised abroad for tolerating the destruction of the Berlin Wall in 1989, Gorbachev's popularity at home fell as his reforms ran into the sand. *Glasnost* assumed a momentum of its own, breaking the Party's monopoly of political power, sparking industrial unrest and unleashing pent-up ethnic tensions.

Instead of using it to resuscitate communism as Gorbachev had hoped, the people took *glasnost* at face value and pressed for ever wider freedoms. At the 1990 May Day parade in Red

SOVIET/RUSSIAN LEADERS 1917–PRESENT

1917–22 Vladimir Ulyanov – 'Lenin'
1922–53 Joseph Djugashvili – 'Stalin'
1953–64 Nikita Khrushchev
1964–82 Leonid Brezhnev
1982–4 Yuri Andropov
1984–5 Konstantin Chernenko
1985–91 Mikhail Gorbachev
1991–9 Boris Yeltsin
2000– Vladimir Putin

The lower house of the Russian Parliament (Duma)

Square, Gorbachev was booed as he stood on Lenin's Mausoleum.

Gorbachev met his nemesis in the democratically elected president of the Russian Republic, Boris Yeltsin, who used his mandate to declare Russian independence in June 1991, forcing Gorbachev to agree to the drafting of a new Union Treaty.

Transition to democracy and back again

Six months later, communism was gone and Russia was in turmoil. It had lost much of its 'empire' and, to make matters worse, fell into a war with breakaway Chechnya which brought criticism from the West. The economy was stagnating and inflation skyrocketed. Those quick enough to take advantage of the confusion were knocked back down by the economic crisis of 1998. All of this cast the experiment with democracy in a bad light and resulted in the return of a more authoritarian type of rule under Yeltsin's successor.

The Putin era

An erstwhile KGB officer from St Petersburg, Vladimir Putin was appointed to take over from Yeltsin at the end of 1999. He called for a strong united Russia, unashamed of its (Soviet) past. Economic liberalisation would continue but with control of large and prosperous industries, most notably oil and gas, de facto back in the hands of the Kremlin. Regional governors were now appointed to rule in the president's name and powerful oligarchs such as Mikhail Khodorkovsky were silenced. Putin was also able to bring the war in Chechnya to a successful but brutal end under the veil of 'counterterrorism' following the 9/11 attacks in the USA.

Putin's tough stance has been popular across the land, winning his party 'United Russia' victory after victory in essentially free and fair elections. The constitution required him to hand over the reins of power to Dmitry Medvedev in 2008 but, by popular consent, he is expected to return as president in the near future.

Politics

Detail from the Duma with the flag of the Russian Federation

Culture

Russians are fiercely proud of their deep cultural heritage, both in the arts and in daily life. Here peasant joie de vivre *meets abstract philosophy, in a culture that has been moulded by centuries of foreign invasion, despotic government and Orthodox piety. There is no better introduction to it than a stay in Moscow or St Petersburg.*

The arts

A love of the arts is by no means an elite diversion in Russia, where concerts and exhibitions are heavily subsidised and the national poet, Alexander Pushkin (1799–1837), is cherished with a passion far exceeding that of the English for Shakespeare or the Germans for Goethe.

Many artists enjoy a kind of cult status generally reserved in the West for pop stars. The reason is simple: under autocratic rule, producing subversive work carried the risk of imprisonment or exile if the tsar was displeased. Likewise, after 1917, artists denied membership of the official state union were liable to imprisonment as 'social parasites'. Their work would be secretly shared with trusted friends late in the evening around the kitchen table.

Russkaya dusha

The 'Russian soul' – *russkaya dusha* – is more legend than fact, some say. At a time when burgers and BMWs are more in demand than balalaikas, the fabled Russian character can seem no deeper than the lacquer on the cheap nesting dolls sold at tourist flea markets.

But as many foreigners will agree, there is a certain quality to chance acquaintances in Moscow and St Petersburg that remains uniquely Russian. The quality is one of contradiction – a cross between public conformity and private dreams of anarchy, ruthless realism combined with sugary sentimentalism, striking rudeness on the street contrasted with overwhelming generosity to guests at home. Russians complain about the price of cabbages and wax lyrical about frost on the hawthorn in the same breath.

The *mir*

One explanation is that most city-dwellers are only two or three generations removed from the countryside and its collectivist traditions. Outsiders are treated with suspicion, insiders are doted on and nonconformists are shunned: the Russian word for 'peasant community' is the same as that for the 'world' – *mir*.

Sometimes the result is plain bigotry. A streak of anti-Semitism runs deep in the national psyche, and even today a vocal element in every political demonstration blames everything from the October Revolution to the price of Coca-Cola on 'Zionist conspirators'.

Belief and superstition

Despite decades of state-sponsored atheism, Russians are, in the widest sense, a strikingly religious people.

The Orthodox Church is in full flourish again, as the shining new bell towers above the cities' rooftops testify. On a different level, from the adoration of Lenin to the post-Soviet fascination with television hypnotists and cure-all medicines, Russians have an unquenchable thirst for the improbable.

Westernisers and Slavophiles

Neither truly a part of Europe nor of Asia, Russia's fate has for centuries been hotly disputed between those who want to modernise the country on Western lines and those who believe in a distinct, Slavic, way forward. Those *zapadniki* ('Westernisers'), such as Peter the Great, who tried to turn Russia towards Europe, often did so with Asian barbarity. Meanwhile, the *slavyanofili* ('Slavophiles') declared Orthodox Russia's messianic role in the world but had no practical plan of action beyond extolling the peasant as a model of social organisation.

Today the nationalists hold sway; eager to see Russia as a revived superpower they have rejected NATO and EU membership in favour of military might and gas-fuelled geopolitics. It will be some time yet before Russia once again flirts with Western-style democracy and reform.

Lenin's Mausoleum in Moscow

Haves and have nots

The Soviet Union was never the land of equality of socialist propaganda, despite the promises of Nikita Khrushchev that communism would be perfected by 1980. But when the system finally disintegrated, people were plunged into a confusing free-for-all. Now a few cruise the streets in Lincolns and Mercedes while the majority struggle desperately to make ends meet.

When artificially controlled prices were freed in 1992, inflation spiralled out of control. A pound sterling bought 140 roubles then; three years later, it bought almost 7,000. A two-tier society emerged and a bankrupt state could do nothing to help the losers: the monthly pension in late 1994 could be as little as 30,000 roubles, or about £6.

Underground stations were thronged with people selling bread, vodka, lottery tickets and ballpoint pens late into the night. Qualified scientists, teachers and doctors

The wealthy citizens of Moscow like to display their wealth

resorted to selling souvenirs at tourist markets or importing cheap Chinese clothing to sell at home.

But the winners became very rich, very quickly. Whether communist-era bureaucrats who retained their posts or mafia-like racketeers, they exploited the chaos of the market, making huge sums exporting oil and raw materials or taking a hefty percentage of business and restaurant turnovers. Russia's new breed of *biznismyen* lost little time in carving up the 'Wild East'.

As elsewhere, the rich get richer and the poor get poorer. In big cities, though, the middle class is increasing. Shops are not just for the rich any more, but frequented by 'ordinary' people, many of whom are becoming quite content. Those who work in foreign or private companies earn decent money in Russian terms, and can afford foreign holidays, one or two cars and a decent living standard.

To be rich in Russia means to be incredibly rich – according to one recent estimate, 25 per cent of the national wealth is in the hands of just 100 individuals, and there are more billionaires in Moscow than anywhere in the world. And while it is true that under President Putin the political power of the tycoons has declined, they still wield enormous economic clout. Remote from ordinary life, they live their lives within the confines

It is difficult not to feel sorry for the homeless children

of luxurious villas and dachas, venturing out only to broker deals or to party with celebrities in exclusive nightclubs.

To be poor in Russia means to be incredibly poor. Many live on the streets due to alcoholism, drug abuse, eviction or unemployment. Unqualified workers have no chance of another job. Pensions are so low that, if old people have no family to take care of them, they have to resort to begging. It is not uncommon to see old men and women wearing medals for heroism while begging on the street corner from people for whose freedom they once fought.

Impressions

It takes a little courage to choose Russia for a holiday. Though the country has more or less learnt how to deal with modern tourism, it still has its strange alphabet, strict bureaucrats and ever-present police checking the documents of passers-by. Yet a thoroughly rewarding trip is well within the grasp of any visitor armed with a sense of humour and a few ground rules.

The price of change

Take personal security seriously. Today's Russia is an exhilarating, brutal and frequently bewildering place and it pays to have your wits about you. Wear a money belt under your clothing and keep cameras and other valuables close to your person. Watch out for pickpockets, especially on the metro and in other crowded places. Give money-changers and other hustlers a wide berth, and – one final precaution – make photocopies of your passport and visa and note down credit card details, including emergency phone numbers, in case of loss.

Moscow and St Petersburg can no longer be regarded as cheap destinations; indeed, Moscow was recently voted the most expensive city in the world. The free market has created a society with a burgeoning middle class, but one in which the disparity in wealth between the very rich and the very poor is vast. For visitors this means expensive hotel bills and restaurant prices on a par with those of London, Paris or New York. Foreigners are also expected to pay well above the local going rate for admission to museums, theatres and other

Renovations are under way on many older buildings

Porters and passengers at Vitebsky Station in St Petersburg

attractions. There are still bargains to be had, however, while some things, notably public transport, remain downright cheap.

After seven years of incredible economic growth, the Russian economy hit the buffers in 2008 and has been affected more than most by the world economic downturn. Factories have made sweeping redundancies, falling oil prices have decimated entire communities, and countless businesses have gone to the wall. The gap between rich and poor remains grotesque and millions of Russians live below the poverty line. Of particular worry are life expectancy, birth rates and an underfunded health service which continues to deteriorate.

When to visit

There can be nothing more Russian than the crisp frosts of winter, ice on the Neva and snow falling upon the golden cupolas of Moscow's churches. Likewise, there can be nothing more unpleasant than permanently frozen fingers and wet feet. To avoid too much of the latter, the best time for a winter trip is late November through to early January before the really heavy frosts or the slush of the March thaw.

In the warmer season, July and August can be suffocating in both

Moscow and St Petersburg. The air is fresher around May and September, and, if the weather holds, these are perhaps the most attractive times of the year. To catch the legendary St Petersburg White Nights, when the sun virtually never sets and the whole city celebrates, plan your trip for the end of June or beginning of July.

Visas and arrival

The vast majority of foreign nationals require a visa to enter Russia which can only be issued on a full passport. Bear in mind when planning your trip that the visa issuing process can still be lengthy, though things have improved in recent years. If organising your own visa, allow plenty of time (ideally a month) before departure. Going through a visa agency adds to the cost but reduces the entire process down to one simple form.

Airport arrivals are not the trial they once were and you can be through Sheremetyevo passport and customs checks quicker than the equivalent at London's Heathrow. Don't forget to fill in an immigration card either on the plane or after landing. One half is taken by the immigration official, the other stays in your passport until you leave. Bring a paperclip to make sure it doesn't fall out.

Taxis are best avoided across the Russian Federation, but this rings doubly true at airports. Fortunately, Moscow's international airports are now linked to the city centre by rail.

Moscow Metro

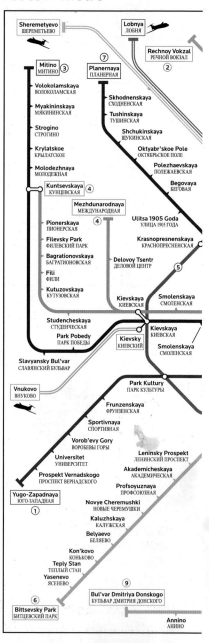

Impressions

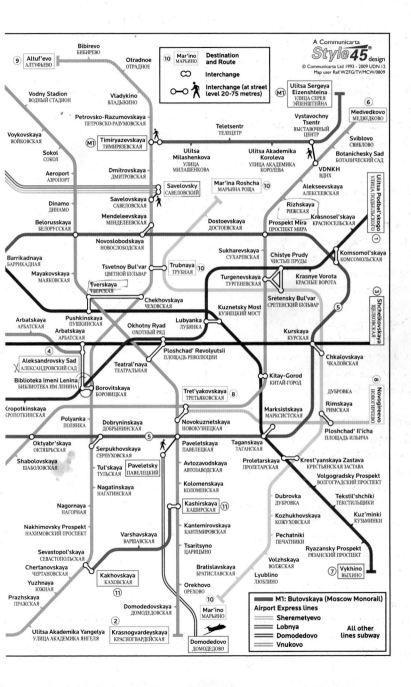

An uplifting mosaic in a Moscow Metro station

Coping with the language

Nothing will increase the pleasure and ease of your trip to Russia more than a few hours at home spent mastering the Cyrillic alphabet. Although the task seems daunting, the value later is immeasurable for working out metro stations and street names (few signs are bilingual in St Petersburg; hardly any are in Moscow). You will also be able to pronounce words and destinations – Russian is basically a phonetic language and most words are spoken just as they are spelt.

A handful of polite words learnt at home will go a long way towards melting the icy glare of even the most unhelpful official.

(*See pp184–5 for an introduction to basic words and phrases.*)

TRANSLITERATION TROUBLE

The Cyrillic alphabet used in Russia contains letters which do not correspond directly to the Roman alphabet (*see pp184–5*). Since there are different ways of transliterating the same letters and sounds, you should not be put off by slight variations in spellings on tourist maps, in travel guides (including this one) and in other English language publications about Russia.

Organising your time

Moscow and St Petersburg offer an astounding range of sights and activities for even the most demanding visitor. You will only be able to cover a fraction of them in the course of a normal trip, so it is worth sorting out priorities in advance. Most of the major sights in both cities are conveniently grouped near the centre; some, such as the Kremlin or the Hermitage, require most of a day to do them justice. Minor points of interest, such as lesser-known museums and churches, are often spread far apart and the travelling involved is easy to underestimate. Don't feel obliged to trudge from one landmark to another – remember to save some enthusiasm for that trip to the ballet, five-course meal or ice-hockey game in the evening!

Orientation

Moscow is planned like a cartwheel with major arteries branching out from the Kremlin (Kreml) and linked by a series of concentric ring roads. The first is the Bulvar (Boulevard Ring), which starts and stops at (but does not cross) the Moskva River, on either side of the Kremlin. The next ring road is the Sadovaya (Garden Ring), a heaving multi-lane highway encircling the city centre. (Note: It does *not* coincide with the circle line of the metro.) The Tretya Koltso (Third Ring) was added in the 1990s.

Finally, the Outer Ring Road (MKAD – Moskovskaya Koltsevaya Avtodoroga) defines the city's limits far on the outskirts of town.

St Petersburg is simpler, with most points of interest grouped on, around or at the ends of Nevskiy Prospekt, the city's backbone.

Driving

Driving around Moscow and St Petersburg is technically possible but not recommended.

Little has changed since the 19th century when the writer Nikolai Gogol observed, 'What Russian does not love fast driving? How could his soul, which is so eager to whirl round and round, to forget everything in a mad carousel, to exclaim sometimes: To hell with it all! ... How could his soul not love it?'

Russians overtake on both sides, aim for gaps in the traffic that do not exist and mercilessly refuse to give way to timid foreign drivers. In addition, the roads are riddled with potholes and

Moscow's transport is very efficient, but working out the routes can be tricky

governed by an extremely arcane highway code.

For the undaunted, there are plenty of car rental agencies in both cities (*see p181 for more information*).

The unpredictable

Economic and political turmoil has added to the ever-present element of unpredictability in Russian life. Prepare to find museums unexpectedly closed for renovation. Do not be surprised if a favourite restaurant slides dramatically downmarket in the course of a week; nor if the exchange rate does the same. Anticipate that booking offices may be closed, as the sign will say, 'for technical reasons'. Be prepared to be denied access to an apparently public bar for not knowing the right people. It is all part of the adventure.

Public transport

As in any city, getting the hang of the public transport system in Moscow and St Petersburg takes practice. While you can conceivably do without using it, a few tactical stops on the metro (underground) network will dramatically save time and energy between sights. Buses, trams and trolleybuses are trickier to master, but where essential, they are mentioned in the text. To begin with, try trolleybuses B and B-red for negotiating Moscow's Garden Ring, while in St Petersburg, Nos 22 and 7 cut out the footwork on Nevskiy Prospekt (*see pp186–8 for detailed information on travelling by public transport*).

St Petersburg Metro

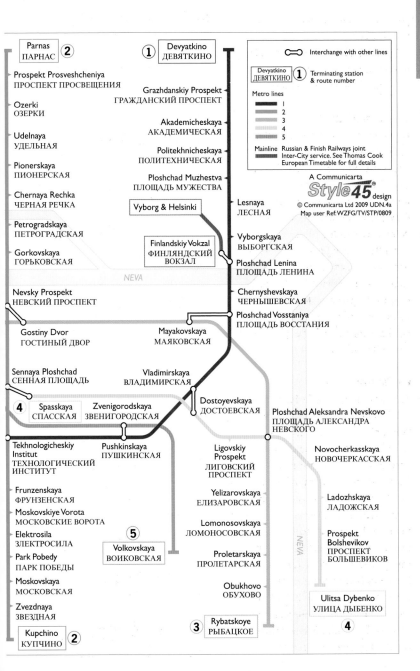

Parnas ② ПАРНАС

① Devyatkino ДЕВЯТКИНО

Prospekt Prosveshcheniya ПРОСПЕКТ ПРОСВЕЩЕНИЯ

Grazhdanskiy Prospekt ГРАЖДАНСКИЙ ПРОСПЕКТ

Ozerki ОЗЕРКИ

Akademicheskaya АКАДЕМИЧЕСКАЯ

Udelnaya УДЕЛЬНАЯ

Politekhnicheskaya ПОЛИТЕХНИЧЕСКАЯ

Pionerskaya ПИОНЕРСКАЯ

Ploshchad Muzhestva ПЛОЩАДЬ МУЖЕСТВА

Chernaya Rechka ЧЕРНАЯ РЕЧКА

Vyborg & Helsinki

Lesnaya ЛЕСНАЯ

Petrogradskaya ПЕТРОГРАДСКАЯ

Finlandskiy Vokzal ФИНЛЯНДСКИЙ ВОКЗАЛ

Vyborgskaya ВЫБОРГСКАЯ

Gorkovskaya ГОРЬКОВСКАЯ

Ploshchad Lenina ПЛОЩАДЬ ЛЕНИНА

NEVA

Nevsky Prospekt НЕВСКИЙ ПРОСПЕКТ

Chernyshevskaya ЧЕРНЫШЕВСКАЯ

Ploshchad Vosstaniya ПЛОЩАДЬ ВОССТАНИЯ

Gostiny Dvor ГОСТИНЫЙ ДВОР

Mayakovskaya МАЯКОВСКАЯ

Sennaya Ploshchad СЕННАЯ ПЛОЩАДЬ

Vladimirskaya ВЛАДИМИРСКАЯ

④ Spasskaya СПАССКАЯ

Zvenigorodskaya ЗВЕНИГОРОДСКАЯ

Dostoyevskaya ДОСТОЕВСКАЯ

Ploshchad Aleksandra Nevskovo ПЛОЩАДЬ АЛЕКСАНДРА НЕВСКОГО

Tekhnologicheskiy Institut ТЕХНОЛОГИЧЕСКИЙ ИНСТИТУТ

Pushkinskaya ПУШКИНСКАЯ

Ligovskiy Prospekt ЛИГОВСКИЙ ПРОСПЕКТ

Novocherkasskaya НОВОЧЕРКАССКАЯ

Frunzenskaya ФРУНЗЕНСКАЯ

Yelizarovskaya ЕЛИЗАРОВСКАЯ

Ladozhskaya ЛАДОЖСКАЯ

Moskovskiye Vorota МОСКОВСКИЕ ВОРОТА

Lomonosovskaya ЛОМОНОСОВСКАЯ

Elektrosila ЭЛЕКТРОСИЛА

⑤ Volkovskaya ВОЛКОВСКАЯ

Prospekt Bolshevikov ПРОСПЕКТ БОЛЬШЕВИКОВ

Park Pobedy ПАРК ПОБЕДЫ

Proletarskaya ПРОЛЕТАРСКАЯ

NEVA

Moskovskaya МОСКОВСКАЯ

Obukhovo ОБУХОВО

Zvezdnaya ЗВЕЗДНАЯ

Ulitsa Dybenko УЛИЦА ДЫБЕНКО

Kupchino ② КУПЧИНО

③ Rybatskoye РЫБАЦКОЕ

④

Interchange with other lines

Devyatkino ДЕВЯТКИНО ① Terminating station & route number

Metro lines
1
2
3
4
5

Mainline Russian & Finish Railways joint Inter-City service. See Thomas Cook European Timetable for full details

A Communicarta
Style 45® design
© Communicarta Ltd 2009 UDN.4a
Map user Ref:WZFG/TV/STP/0809

Moskva (Moscow)

'Moscow! How much is combined in this sound for the Russian heart!' wrote the national poet, Alexander Pushkin in the 19th century. The city is the capital and one of the cultural focuses of Russia, enshrining civic ceremony and the Orthodox faith, great musical traditions and theatrical excellence. Most of all, it is the incarnation of that subtle blend of anarchy and nostalgia which the nation proudly refers to as the 'Russian Soul'.

A fight for survival

Since its humble inception in 1147 as a small encampment overlooking the Moskva River, Moscow has suffered frequent attack. First came the Mongols – or Tartars – who sacked the city, gathered slaves and collected tribute from the residents. Fear of the 'Tartar yoke' lasted until the 16th century – they last levelled the city in 1571. Next came the Poles, who occupied the city for two years at the beginning of the following century.

The Historical Museum on Red Square

Relative peace then ensued as St Petersburg assumed the mantle of Imperial capital until, in 1812, Napoleon entered the Kremlin. A desperate population resorted to setting the city ablaze to drive him out. Finally, in 1941, Hitler boasted: 'In a few weeks, we shall be in Moscow. I will raze that damned city and in its place construct an artificial lake with central lighting.' He failed.

The old and the new

As capital of the Soviet Union, Moscow grew rapidly from a picturesque, medieval city into a sprawling, modern metropolis. Soviet planners blasted away old quarters of the city to erect massive hotels and force through multi-lane highways. Stalin ordered the construction of the vast Gothic skyscrapers that today dominate the skyline.

But Moscow retains plenty of its old character and remains a Russian, rather than Soviet, city. Whole streets are lined

Moscow town plan

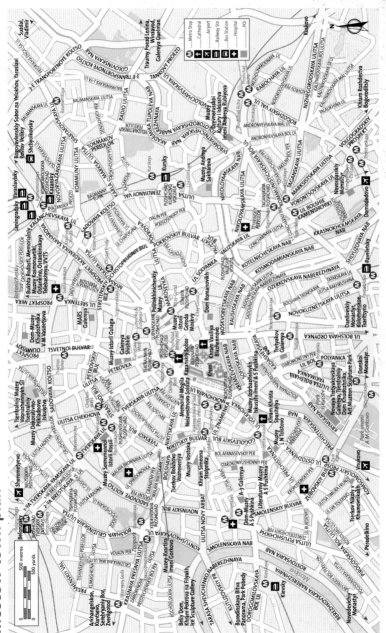

🚇	Metro Stop
✝	Cathedral
✈	Airport
🚂	Railway Stn
🚌	Bus Station
✚	Hospital
■	POI

Suzdal, Vladimir

Traumy Poezd Lenina, Winzavod, Galereya Guelman

TANKVY PROEZD

GOLOVINSKAYA NAB

3-E TRANSPORTNOE KOLTSO

Koskovo

Sheremetyevo

Belorussky

0   500 metres
0   500 yards

with the neoclassical mansions of the old aristocracy. Wandering into a back alley off the main roads can be like entering a time warp as you stumble across delicate Orthodox churches and courtyards little changed from the time of Tolstoy and Dostoevsky.

The Muscovites

Russia is a land of over 100 separate nationalities, from Tuvans to Kalmyks and Chukchi to Circassians, as well as the Russians themselves. A true Muscovite is a rare individual indeed. But whatever their origin, the ten million or so inhabitants of Moscow are proud of their city, for all its eccentricities and hardships.

Some say that Muscovites unjustly perceive themselves as the nation's top crop. Whether this is true or not, visitors must judge for themselves. As Muscovites like to say, there are Russians and there are Muscovites.

KREMLIN, KITAY-GOROD AND ZAMOSKVORECHE
Aleksandrovskiy Sad (Alexander Gardens)

Tucked under the Kremlin's western wall, the Alexander Gardens are best known for the solemn Tomb of the Unknown Soldier. The gardens were laid out for Tsar Alexander I in 1821 over the bricked-in Neglinnaya River – which might account for the characteristic coolness they afford in summer after a hot afternoon's visit to the Kremlin.

Manezhnaya Ulitsa. Free admission. Metro: Aleksandrovskiy Sad/Biblioteka imeni Lenina.

Borovitskaya Ploshchad (Borovitskiy Square)

Adjoining the southern end of the gardens, this busy intersection is dominated by the striking Pashkov Dom (Pashkov House), built between 1784 and 1786. It now shares some of the 29 million volumes of the neighbouring Biblioteka imeni Lenina (Lenin Library), Europe's largest library in terms of book numbers.

Old Russian architecture paid a lot of attention to detail

DIEHARD COMMUNISTS

The statue of Karl Marx opposite the Bolshoi
Theatre and the former Lenin Museum on
Ploshchad Revolyutsii are favourite gathering
points of diehard communists (*metro:
Ploshchad Revolyutsii*). Mostly pensioners,
the true believers are now more of a tourist
sight than a real political force.
Demonstrations take place most Sundays,
but the really big crowds gather on 7
November (Revolution Day), May Day and
Victory Day (9 May).

Manezhnaya Ploshchad
(Manezh Square)

The low, columned building alongside
the upper half of the gardens is the
former Imperial Riding School, or
Manezh. Destroyed by fire in March
2004, it has since been rebuilt and is
open for exhibitions (*see also p35*).

Memorial Mogila Neizvestnovo Soldata
(The Tomb of the Unknown Soldier)

The memory of World War II is deeply
felt in Russia. Estimated at 27 million,
the number of Soviet deaths will never
be precisely known. Official delegations
and newlyweds lay wreaths on the grave
of an infantryman killed at the 41km
(25½-mile) point on Leningradskoye
Shosse (Leningrad Highway), the
closest German soldiers came to
Moscow. The inscription beneath the
eternal flame reads: 'Your name is
unknown, your deeds immortal'.

Obelisk

Under Lenin's orders, the first of
countless memorials to the Revolution
was unveiled in the Alexander Gardens
in 1918. It was previously a monument
celebrating the tercentenary of the
Romanov dynasty, but the Bolsheviks
knocked off the double-headed
eagle and inscribed the names of
socialist thinkers.

Dom Romanovikh
(Romanov House)

Built by the grandfather of Tsar
Mikhail, the first of the Romanov
dynasty, this elegant city residence has
been restored as a museum of 16th-
and 17th-century aristocratic life.
*Ulitsa Varvarka 10. Tel: 495 692 1256.
Open: Mon, Thur 10am–5pm, Wed
11am–6pm. Closed: first Mon of month.
Admission charge.
Metro: Ploshchad Revolyutsii.*

The Tomb of the Unknown Soldier with its
Guard of Honour

Walk: From the Lubyanka to Manezhnaya Ploshchad

Sometimes overlooked, this route between Kitay-Gorod and the centre runs from the old headquarters of communist oppression to the new one of free trade. Those with good legs or those short of time may make it one long walk from Kitay-Gorod to Gorky Park.

Allow 1¹/₂ hours for this walk excluding visits to shopping centres or the Manezh.

Start at Lubyanka metro.

1 The Lubyanka

The large building on Lubyanskaya Square, by the architect Aleksey Shchusev, is known as the Lubyanka.

Rumour suggests the Lubyanka is as big below ground as above. The headquarters of the notorious KGB had a jail, death row and possibly torture chambers, for those who dared oppose the communist regime. Many who

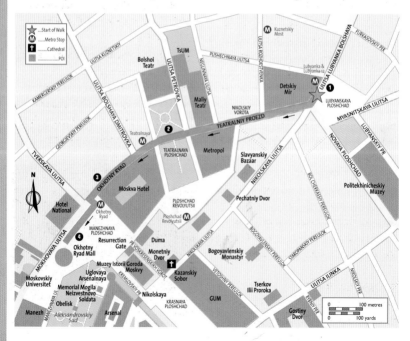

entered it were never seen again, and many more were sent to labour camps in Siberia – a sentence equal to death, since few returned alive.

The Lubyanka today belongs to the FSB, successor of the KGB in the democratic state (*see pp58–9*). *Proceed down towards the centre, along Teatralniy Proezd, until you reach the large Teatralnaya Ploshchad.*

2 Teatralnaya Ploshchad

On this square stands one of the world's best-known theatres, the Bolshoi, one of the largest in Europe and famous for its opera and ballet performances. It is a fine example of Russian 19th-century architecture, designed by Osip Bove and Andrey Mikhailov (*see pp152–3*).

Teatralnaya Ploshchad has two more theatres – the Children's Theatre and the Small (Maliy) Theatre. Also interesting is the Hotel Metropol, built in the early 20th century in modernist style and well worth a look inside.

Opposite the Bolshoi is a statue of Karl Marx, whom communists see as the founder of communism and socialism. This is one of the last communist-era statues in the city that remains in its original spot, and diehard communists still meet here. *Continue in the same direction to Okhotny Ryad and Manezhnaya Ploshchad.*

3 Okhotny Ryad

Once an area of small town houses, this is now one of the most highly commercial parts of Moscow. Notable buildings are the Russian Duma (lower house of parliament) and the Hotel National. Okhotny Ryad is better known for its three-level shopping centre. Its cupola showing the northern hemisphere merges well with the fountains in the square above.

4 Manezhnaya Ploshchad

The foot of this square is dominated by the Hotel Moscow and it reaches to the Manezh exhibition hall opposite. The arena, built in 1817 for the visit of Alexander I, blends simplicity with monumentality. After the tsar's visit, it was used as the Imperial Riding School. Today it is the venue for national and international exhibitions. Its floor area of 6,500sq m (70,000sq ft), almost as big as Christ the Saviour Cathedral, is astonishing.

The square did not exist until the 1930s. It runs alongside the Aleksandrovskiy Sad, close to the Kremlin, Red Square and Tverskaya Ulitsa. Visitors to Moscow tend to fall in love with this square and keep coming back to it.

A fountain on Manezhnaya Ploshchad

The Moscow Metro

Moscow's metro system is reputedly the world's most efficient but also rates as a must-see among the capital's tourist sights. Many of the stations are architecturally as stunning as anything above ground, and a tour of this bizarre subterranean commuter world costs no more than an ordinary ticket from a machine.

Underground palaces

At 7am on 15 May 1935, Mr Lakyshev of the Red Proletariat factory bought a ticket at Sokolniki station and became the first of over 77 billion passengers to ride Moscow's celebrated metro. The metro was planned by Stalin as a showpiece of communist engineering capable of transporting the city's workers rapidly and in the lap of socialist luxury. The older stations are the most impressive, heavily decorated with Stalinist-Baroque marble, stucco, crystal and works of Socialist Realist art. New stations, in contrast, are a study in soulless modernity. Throughout the 20th century Russia exported its building techniques and rolling stock to other parts of the USSR and Eastern Europe.

A pick of the stations

Kievskaya: designed to celebrate the friendship of the Russian and Ukrainian peoples, the mosaics were completed at a time when forced collectivisation by Stalin killed millions in the Ukraine.

Komsomolskaya: honouring Soviet youth, this palace of gold, marble and florid stucco depicts scenes from Russian history.

Mayakovskaya: completed in 1938 to a prize-winning design by Aleksey Dushkin, the station is named after the poet and playwright Vladimir Mayakovsky (1893–1930). Features to look out for include the mosaics on the theme of aviation and sport.

Park Kultury: originally the terminus of the Sokolniki line, the bas-reliefs depict workers at leisure, playing chess, skating, reading and dancing.

Ploshchad Revolyutsii: this station celebrates the Great October Revolution of 1917 with 36 heroic bronze figures, paired under each of its 40 arches. They depict the major contributors to the founding of the Soviet state, from sailors and young pioneers to architects and sportsmen.

Mind-boggling stats

Every day 631 escalators at 177 stations carry over 9 million

An elegant interior typical of Moscow's metro stations

passengers to 9,915 trains that travel 292km (182 miles) of track and consume almost 5 million kWh of electricity. The system is operated by a whopping 34,792 employees and runs punctually over 99 per cent of the time. New track and stations open every year, meaning these amazing figures just rise and rise!

Wartime metro

Constructed to double up as vast air-raid shelters, many of the stations are extremely deep underground (this may be the longest escalator ride you are ever likely to take). In 1941 Stalin addressed deputies in Mayakovskaya station on the anniversary of the Revolution and had an office at Chistye Prudy in the Air Defence Command outpost – reached by a secret door behind the bust of Kirov.

Besides the metro, Moscow is riddled with other tunnels. Some link with the former KGB headquarters, while those beneath the White House and the Kremlin are reported to be wide enough to drive a car through.

Travelling the metro

First buy a magnetic ticket from a machine or kiosk then pass through the turnstile. Trains are pretty frequent so you'll not wait long. On crowded trains, passengers behind you wishing to get off may ask you if you're doing likewise. It's bad form just to push your way through the throng. Getting on a train while people are alighting is accepted; younger passengers are expected to give up their seats to the elderly.

Iconostasis in the Don Monastery church

were believed to have helped defeat the Crimean Tartars. The original icon is now in the Tretyakov Gallery (*see pp54–5*). Today the monastery is once again operative.

Donskaya Ploshchad 1. Tel: 495 232 0221. Open: daily 7am–dusk. Metro: Shabolovskaya.

Krasnaya Ploshchad (Red Square)

Witness to holy processions, executions, grandiose military parades and bloody insurrections, the vast, cobbled expanse of Red Square is the spiritual heart of both capital and nation. At the far end, the visitor's eye is drawn by the fantastic cupolas of St Basil's Cathedral, quintessential symbol of Moscow.

A bustling marketplace in early times, the square saw Ivan the Terrible beg forgiveness for his misdeeds and Peter the Great personally undertake

Donskoi Monastyr (Don Monastery)

Patriarch Tikhon was kept under arrest by the Bolsheviks in the monastery's Old Cathedral, where his tomb now lies. The Don Monastery is also the resting place of many of Moscow's aristocrats, including the wealthy Golitsyn family, who are buried in the Church of the Archangel Michael in the monastery grounds.

The oldest buildings and fortress walls date from the 16th century when the monastery was founded by Boris Godunov in honour of the Don Mother of God icon, whose miraculous powers

MOSCOW'S CONFUSING TELEPHONE CODES

Moscow's telephone system seems to have been in perpetual chaos since the fall of communism and recent changes have seen further disarray. Basically there are now two area prefixes, 495 and 499. Many numbers are changing code as well as undergoing slight alteration to the first few digits. Within the 495 area you don't need to dial any prefix. Within the 499 code area the prefix must be dialled. From one area to another you must dial 8 then the city code (495 or 499). In this guide we have included the area code with each number. No such problems afflict St Petersburg.

the beheading of his foes. *Krasnaya* in old Russian meant 'beautiful', and it is only recently that the square became identified with 'red' communism.
Metro: Ploshchad Revolyutsii/ Okhotny Ryad.

GUM

Privatised, and officially known as the 'Upper Trading Rows', this glorious shopping arcade opposite the Kremlin is still affectionately known by its Soviet acronym, standing for 'State Department Store'. Completed in 1888, its bridges and balconies afford a bird's-eye view of the shopping frenzy below.

Kazanskiy Sobor (Kazan Cathedral)

Constructed in 1636 in honour of the miraculous 'Mother of God of Kazan' icon that helped rid Muscovy of the Poles, Kazan Cathedral was destroyed by Stalin 300 years later to erect public toilets. Detailed plans kept in secret were used to rebuild it. The patriarch blessed it in 1993.
Open: daily 8am–7pm.

Khram Vasiliya Blazhennovo (St Basil's Cathedral)

Napoleon referred to the cathedral as 'that mosque' and stabled his horses here during the invasion of 1812. Whatever one's taste, there is no denying the motley splendour of the Cathedral of the Intercession of the Virgin, better known as St Basil's after

the 'holy fool' famed for his denunciation of Ivan the Terrible and buried in one of the chapels.

Ivan decreed work on the building to begin following the capture of the Khanate of Kazan: legend has it that he had the architects' eyes put out on completion in 1555 to prevent them creating anything more beautiful.

The central chapel reaches a height of 57m (187ft) and the surrounding eight

Kazan Cathedral on Red Square

are built to a strict geometric design. The exterior was originally white and gold, the present vivid colour scheme being added in the 17th century. The interior is more understated, but it is well worth wandering the convoluted corridors to see the recently restored frescos and icons.

Tel: 495 698 3304.
Open: Wed–Mon 11am–5pm.
Closed: first Mon of month.
Admission charge.

St Basil's Cathedral at the lower end of Red Square is probably the most photographed sight in Moscow

Lobnoe Mesto

While the origins of the name are unclear, the history of Muscovy's ancient tribune is dramatic. In 1613, the first of the Romanov dynasty, Mikhail, was here proclaimed tsar; the leader of the 1682 peasants' revolt, Stenka Razin, was led along the street now bearing his name to be quartered on the site; and Peter the Great reputedly executed the first ten of the 2,000 rebellious palace guard here in 1698.

Mavzoley V I Lenina
(Lenin's Mausoleum)

A week after his death, Lenin's wife, Krupskaya, wrote to *Pravda* imploring: 'Do not build memorials to him or palaces to his name. Do not organise pompous ceremonies in his memory.' Her pleas went unanswered and the result is the granite and porphyry ziggurat, designed by the distinguished Soviet architect Aleksey Shchusev.

Bedecked in a polka-dot bow tie, Lenin is maintained in his crystal sarcophagus by a computer-controlled ventilation system and a yearly bathing with a chemical cocktail. The honour guard at the gates was abolished by Yeltsin, but changing political fortunes have put on hold plans to clear the site. Thousands of old communists still gather here on 22 April to celebrate their idol's birthday.

The Kremlin wall behind the building is the ex-USSR's principal necropolis. Here, with Stalin and other Bolshevik luminaries, lie Yuri Gagarin, the first man in space, and the American chronicler of the Revolution, John Reed. Before entering the mausoleum, leave your camera and any bags at the State History Museum.
Krasnaya Ploshchad. Tel: 495 623 5527. Open: Tue–Thur, Sat–Sun 10am–1pm. Free admission.

Minin-Pozharskiy

The statue outside St Basil's depicts the Nizhniy Novgorod butcher Minin persuading Prince Pozharskiy to lead the army to Moscow and drive out the occupying Poles. It was commissioned in a flush of nationalism after 1812. Reliefs show the collection of funds and final surrender of the Poles in 1612.

Nulevoy Kilometr (Zero Kilometre)

In front of the rebuilt Resurrection Gate to Red Square is the 'zero kilometre' plaque. From here all Russian roads are measured. Visitors drop coins on it to ensure safe travel in Russia.

Spasskaya (The Saviour's Tower)

Broadcast on the radio at daybreak, midday and midnight, the bells of the Saviour's Tower, erected in 1491, defined the Soviet worker's day. Under Stalin, the *Internationale* chimed out over Red Square. The small tower alongside was built for Ivan the Terrible so that he could watch executions in comfort.

Walk: Kitay-Gorod

The financial heart of Moscow until the Revolution, Kitay-Gorod is one of the longest-inhabited parts of the capital and largely escaped the brutal Soviet town planning of the 1930s. Impregnable battlements and proximity to the Kremlin attracted artisans' guilds in the Middle Ages, while the concentration of wealth and strict monastic orders played their part in establishing Russia's first centre of learning.

Allow 1¹/₂ hours.

Start at Lubyanka metro and head down Teatralniy Proezd to the Nikolskiy Gates.

1 Nikolskiy Vorota (Nikolskiy Gates)

This is the last remaining of seven former gateways in the mighty walls around Kitay-Gorod. The name of the

stronghold probably derives from the wooden laths (*kiti*) built into the walls for strength.

Head through the arch and turn right along Nikolskaya Ulitsa. The Slavyanskiy Bazaar restaurant at No 7 was a favourite haunt of Russian literati, including the writer Chekhov, the theatre director Stanislavsky and the composers Rimsky-Korsakov and Tchaikovsky.

2 The Russian Renaissance

An elaborate stucco façade decorates the turquoise building at No 15, erected in Russian Gothic style on the site of the former Synodal Printing House (Pechatniy Dvor). Here in 1564 Ivan Fedorov set the type of *The Acts of the Apostles*, Russia's first book. Further down the street in the courtyard of No 9 is another crucible of the Russian Renaissance, the 17th-century Zaikonospasskiy Monastery. The greenish building at the back of the yard was the Slavic-Greek-Latin Academy, Russia's first

university. The Spasskiy Sobor (Saviour's Cathedral), once one of the greatest examples of Russian Baroque architecture, suffered use as a dormitory for metro engineers and a dog-lovers' club under the Soviets.
Retrace your steps and turn right down Bogoyavlenskiy Pereulok.

3 Financial Moscow

Facing you at the end of the street is the classical portico of the former Stock Exchange (*birzha*) building, now the Chamber of Commerce (Torgovaya Palata). Beside it on Ulitsa Ilinka and Rybniy Pereulok stands what was once the mercantile heart of Russia, the Old Merchants' Chambers or Gostiny Dvor, marketplace of traders from all over the empire.

Heading left along Ulitsa Ilinka, note the imposing black façade of the Ministry of Finance at No 9. No 27 is the grandiose premises of the Northern Insurance Society, now home to Russia's Constitutional Court.
Turn right along Staraya Ploshchad (see p65), then right into Nikitnikov Pereulok before turning right down Ipatevskiy Pereulok.

4 Tserkov Troitsy v Nikitnikakh (Church of the Trinity in Nikitniki)

The delicate red-and-white spade gables contribute to the beauty of one of Moscow's most celebrated churches, completed in 1653. The frescos and iconostasis are largely the work of the master Simon Ushakov.

Retrace your steps to the top of Ipatevskiy Per and turn right on to Ulitsa Varvarka.

5 Ulitsa Varvarka

This street of glorious little churches miraculously escaped demolition prior to the construction of the Stalinist-era Hotel Rossiya. Demolition work began on the hotel in 2006 but as yet it is unclear what will replace it.

At No 12 rise the five indigo cupolas studded with gold stars of the 17th-century Tserkov Georgiya (Church of St George), now a shop selling folk arts and crafts. Next door is the Romanov House, built by Mikhail Romanov's grandfather (*see p33*).

The simple Tserkov Maksima Blazhennovo (Church of St Maxim the Blessed) stands at No 6, while the 16th-century Angliyskoe Podvore (English Residence), donated by Ivan the Terrible to members of the London Muscovy Company, is at No 4a. The street comes to an end with the pastel exterior of the classical Tserkov Varvary Velikomuchenitsy (Church of St Barbara).

The elegant façade of the Old Merchants' Chambers

Khram Khrista Spasitelya

Being next to the Kremlin and the largest cathedral in Moscow, Khram Khrista Spasitelya (Cathedral of Christ the Saviour) is hard to overlook. It was originally built to commemorate the defeat of Napoleon in 1812 and work began in 1839. There were a number of sites that were considered for this cathedral, but Tsar Nicholas I chose the hill above the Moskva River. Before construction work could commence, Alekseyevskiy Convent and the Church of all Saints had to be removed from the site. Consecrated on 26 May 1883, the coronation day of Alexander III, it was 103m (338ft) high and its rich interior covered 6,805sq m (73,250sq ft) and could hold 10,000 people. The main dome was 25.5m (84ft) across.

It survived the Revolution, but its central position on a hill overlooking the river was too good to ignore. In 1931 it was torn down on Stalin's orders for one of his megalomaniac projects, a Palace of the Soviets. This palace was meant to be the highest building in the world and was to become a monument to Lenin and the victory of socialism. Massive propaganda preceded the destruction of the cathedral where the communist regime marked it as 'totally inartistic'

and 'misplaced'. In the end the palace was never started and a swimming pool was built instead, but this was plagued by problems and later closed.

After the fall of communism, the mayor of Moscow led the project to erect a replica of Khram Khrista Spasitelya, using modern materials and methods. It has become Moscow's main cathedral, visited by leading public figures and thousands of tourists. The cornerstone for the new cathedral was laid in 1990 and construction work and work on the frescos lasted through to 1999, when the cathedral was consecrated once again.

The cathedral interior holds three altars. The main altar is dedicated to the Birth of Our Lord and the two side altars to St Nicholas and Alexander Nevskiy. One main distinction between the 'new' and the 'old' cathedral is that the 'new' cathedral is placed on a crypt that replaced the initial hill it stood on. Inside the crypt are the Church of Holy Transfiguration, the Hall of Church Councils, the Hall of the Holy Synod, several dining halls, a patriarchal suite, and offices and garages for church staff.

Entry is free, but visitors are expected to behave appropriately (*see p66*). The park around the cathedral has many benches where you can rest your legs while watching ships on the Moskva River.

Tel: 495 202 4734. www.xxc.ru.
Open: daily 10am–5pm.
Free admission. Metro:
Kropotkinskaya.

The majestic Cathedral of Christ the Saviour dominating and overlooking the Moskva River

Kreml (The Kremlin)

All highways in Russia lead to the gates of this, the very hub of imperial and, latterly, Soviet might. To the visitor it is an unnerving place, where the sublime beauty of a medieval cathedral coexists with the terror of a historic torture tower.

The Kremlin dates back to 1156, shortly after Moscow was founded. In 1367, Prince Dmitri Donskoi pulled down the wooden bailey and erected limestone battlements. These were replaced in the late 15th century by vast walls, up to 19m (62ft) high and 6.5m (21ft) wide. Commissioned by Tsar Ivan III ('The Great'), they are the work of Italian architects who were assisted in their labours by Russian craftsmen.

The heart of the Kremlin is the flag-stoned expanse of Sobornaya Ploshchad (Cathedral Square), the spiritual focus of Imperial Russia. Site of royal weddings, coronations and christenings, it is the final resting place of many of the tsars.

A view of the Kremlin from the riverbank

Open: Fri–Wed 9.30am–5pm. Tel: 495 202 3776. www.kremlin.museum.ru. Admission charge. Enter through the Kutafya Tower in the Alexander Gardens (tour groups through the Borovitskiy Gate). Note that the entire Kremlin closes with little warning for state occasions. Guidebooks and audio guides are available from the ticket office. If you hire a local guide (many of them stand around the entrance to the Kremlin) they may help obtain 'sold-out' tickets to the Armoury and Diamond Fund. *Metro: Aleksandrovskiy Sad.*

Admission to the cathedrals is included in the general ticket to the Kremlin.

Arkhangelskiy Sobor (Cathedral of the Archangel Michael)

Dedicated to the patron of the Princes of Muscovy, the cathedral was built in 1508. A team of over 100 artists from all over the kingdom was enlisted to paint the frescos of ancient Russian warriors. Several early tsars are entombed here, including Mikhail, first of the Romanovs, and Ivan the Terrible (the latter out of sight behind the iconostasis, since he was excommunicated by the patriarch).

Blagoveshchenskiy Sobor (Cathedral of the Annunciation)

Built in 1489, the tsars' private church, paved with jasper and capped with nine cupolas, contains 16th-century biblical frescos and one of Russia's most precious iconostases. From the chapel to the right, Ivan the Terrible, forbidden by Orthodox law to enter the church itself, watched proceedings through a partition.

Bolshoi Kremlevskiy Dvorets (Great Kremlin Palace)

Overlooking the river, the tsars' Moscow residence was built for Nicholas I in 1849. The royal apartments have been preserved in pre-revolutionary splendour. Communist leaders lay in state in the Georgievskiy Zal (St George's Hall). Restricted access.

Dvorets Syezdov (State Kremlin Palace)

The key speeches of Gorbachev's *perestroika* were delivered in the 6,000-seat auditorium of this fiercely modern building (1961), also used as a second venue for the Bolshoi opera and ballet.

Granovitaya Dvorets (Palace of Facets)

The squat Palace of Facets (1491) once formed part of the Grand Duke of

The Kremlin

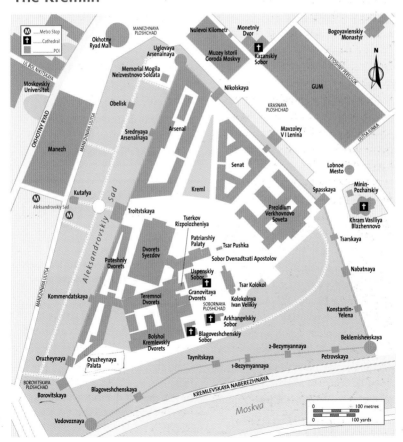

The world's largest cannon – Tsar Pushka

created by Carl Fabergé for the tsar's family. An additional fee grants entrance to the State Diamond Fund, a collection of some of the world's most fantastic gemstones.

The Armoury is closest to the Borovitskaya Gates entrance. Tours daily 10am, noon, 2.30pm, 4.30pm. Admission by separate ticket.

Muscovy's stone residence. It was later used as a banqueting hall and the venue for the celebrated transvestite balls held by the wildly extravagant Empress Elizabeth (reigned 1741–61). Restricted access.

Kolokolnya Ivan Velikiy (Ivan the Great Bell Tower)

For long the tallest structure in Moscow, the 81m (266ft)-high Ivan the Great Bell Tower (1600) dominates Cathedral Square. The tower commands a 40km (25-mile) view across the capital yet its foundations are little more than 4m (13ft) deep. It was initially part of Tserkov Ioana Lestvichnika (Church of St John Climacus). Today 18 of the original 36 bells remain.

Oruzheynaya Palata (The Armoury)

One of the high points of a Kremlin tour is the fabulous wealth on show in the Armoury building. There is a stunning exhibition of treasures such as the battle helmet of Mikhail, first of the Romanov dynasty, and the ivory throne of Ivan the Terrible. Seize the chance to see the collection of jewelled Easter eggs

Patriarshiy Palaty and Sobor Dvenadtsati Apostolov (Patriarch's Palace and Cathedral of the Twelve Apostles)

The palace is now a Museum of 17th Century Life and Applied Art with a superb display of period furniture, gold and silverware and ornate church vestments rescued from Kremlin monasteries destroyed by Stalin. At the end of the exhibition is the tiny Cathedral of the Twelve Apostles.

VLADIMIR ILYICH ULYANOV – 'LENIN' (1870–1924)

Born in the southern city of Simbirsk (now Ulyanovsk), Lenin took up radical politics in earnest after his brother was executed for attempting to assassinate the tsar. Much of his life was spent exiled in Europe, quarrelling in cafés with the many other émigré socialists. He looked 'more like a provincial grocer than a leader of men' according to one British agent, but what marked Lenin out from the rest was his genius for seizing the moment. Smuggled into Russia by the Germans during World War I, he and his tiny 'Bolshevik' ('Majority') party grabbed power in more of a farcical coup than a revolution. As his partner Leon Trotsky remarked, 'Power was lying in the streets.' Lenin simply picked it up.

Prezidium Verkhovnovo Soveta, Senat and Arsenal (Praesidium of the Supreme Soviet, the Senate and the Arsenal)

To the left as you look from the State Kremlin Palace is the 18th-century state Arsenal. Over 800 captured French cannon ring the building's pediment.

In the centre stands the former Senate building (1787), once headquarters of the Soviet government and now housing the presidential administration. To the right is the former Praesidium of the Supreme Soviet.

Teremnoi Dvorets (Terem Palace)

This is perhaps the Kremlin's most spectacular building. The interior seems to owe more to fairytale Baghdad than 17th-century Moscow with its low vaulted ceilings, lavish gilding, ornate tilework and stained-glass windows. Restricted access.

Towers

Of the Kremlin's 20 towers, the Konstantin-Yelena Tower was a torture

Cathedral of the Assumption

chamber and the Blagoveshchenskaya (Annunciation) Tower was used as a prison. The small Tsarskaya (Tsar's) Tower beside the Spasskaya Gates used to be a wooden pavilion from which Ivan the Terrible watched executions on Red Square. The rotating red stars atop each of the towers, made from rubies from the Ural mountains, were erected in 1937 in place of the tsarist two-headed eagle.

Tsar Kolokol and Tsar Pushka (Tsar Bell and Cannon)

The Tsar Bell – at 210 tonnes the world's largest – was cast in 1735 but proved too heavy to hoist and was never rung.

Similarly, the Tsar Cannon, intended to defend the Kremlin's Spasskaya Gates, was never fired. Cast in 1586, it boasts an 890mm calibre.

Tserkov Rizpolozheniya (Church of the Deposition of the Robe)

A private chapel, this church (1655) is decorated with 17th-century frescos and holds a small woodcarving museum.

Uspenskiy Sobor (Cathedral of the Assumption or Dormition)

The cathedral (1479) houses the tombs of all the patriarchs up to 1700. Look for the Throne of Monomakh made for Ivan the Terrible.

In 1989 the cathedral held the first religious service in the Kremlin since 1918.

Street life

Russian cities are a source of contrast, but life on the streets is not as squalid as it was. Gone are the days when every hotel entrance was crowded by beggars, illegal money-changers, pickpockets and crooks. The homeless and street urchins are hardly seen; if they do appear they tend not to bother strangers. Old women begging near churches are tolerated and even pitied.

Since the fall of communism, things have improved for most people in the cities: wages have gone up a little and people seem more content despite the recent economic downturn. They have also got used to foreign visitors: today, central Moscow is full of tourists, diplomats and students. City streets no longer display much of the chaos and poverty of the post-communist years.

The bustling Arbat

Now they are a place where life can be enjoyed to the full. In summer, streets are dotted with beer- or coffee-gardens, many providing live music until late at night. People relax by taking long walks through the city centre, and resting on park benches or next to fountains. Street entertainment is alive and well, with musicians playing anything from Tchaikovsky to modern rock.

Street traders offering 'genuine' war medals, icons, souvenirs and bootleg CDs are an endangered species, however. They have all been forced to move to official markets, partly by city regulations and partly because Russians have taken to the Western concept of huge, air-conditioned shopping centres.

People also breathe more easily on Moscow's boulevards, which now differ little from those of Western cities. It is an unforgettable and romantic experience to sit in a restaurant's garden near the historic walls of the Kremlin and listen to a band playing your favourite songs. The atmosphere – combined with the mellowness of a late Moscow evening and good food and drink – is amazing.

Moscow's roads may have improved, but its traffic has rules of its own and they are quite puzzling for those who do not know them. The main rule is that there are no

Muscovites head for a park at every opportunity they get

rules. However, pedestrian tunnels are frequent and they offer perfect acoustics for street musicians and outdoor studios for portrait painters. Street life seems to have come out of its cocoon.

The transformation to a cosmopolitan capital is complete. Services for foreigners are offered at almost every street corner. The city centre is safe even in the evening and there are many police officers on the streets. All the same, Moscow is a metropolis and has a high crime rate, so adequate caution is advised.

Walk: Zamoskvoreche

Translating as 'Beyond the Moscow River', this area was the city's wild frontier in the Middle Ages, a densely forested region manned by isolated Cossack outposts on the main highway to the settlements of the dreaded Tartar Khans. Subsequently, Moscow's gentry chose Zamoskvoreche for their city estates, and the classical mansions and graceful churches ideally complement a visit to the main attraction, the Tretyakov Gallery.

Allow 2 hours, excluding the Tretyakov Gallery. Start from Oktyabrskaya metro.

1 Kaluzhskaya Ploshchad (formerly October Square)

A colossal statue of Lenin dominates this square. Moving down Ulitsa Bolshaya Yakimanka (to Lenin's right), note the fanciful French Embassy, built at the turn of the 20th century in a pastiche Old Russian style.

Opposite rise the chequered cupolas of the early 18th-century Tserkov Muchenika Ioanna Voyna (Church of St John the Warrior).
Turn right down Khvostov Pereulok to Ulitsa Bolshaya Polyanka.

2 Ulitsa Bolshaya Polyanka

Facing you as you join Ulitsa Bolshaya Polyanka is the 1695 Tserkov Uspeniya (Church of the Dormition). Down the street is the 17th-century Tserkov Grigoriya (Church of St Gregory).
Retrace your steps 50m (55yds) and turn down peaceful Staromonetniy Pereulok,

turn left and then take the second right into Bolshoi Tolmachevskiy Pereulok.

3 Around the Tretyakovskaya

On the right of the street at No 3 stands one of Moscow's finest classical mansions, built in 1770 for the Siberian mining magnate Demidov. On the left is the Church of St Nicholas, now part of the Tretyakov Gallery (*see pp54–5*).
Walk ahead to Ulitsa Bolshaya Ordynka and head right to No 34.

4 Marfo-Mariinskaya Obitel (Convent of Sts Martha and Mary)

Grand Duchess Yelizaveta Fedorovna founded this convent in 1908 after her husband, the governor of Moscow, was blown up by a revolutionary's bomb. The grand duchess's cells house the laundry of a hospital now occupying the grounds. She was executed, like other members of the royal family, in 1918.
Return towards the centre along Ulitsa Bolshaya Ordynka.

5 Ulitsa Bolshaya Ordynka

In the 14th century this was the chief road along which the Tartar horde invaded Moscow. The churches and pre-revolutionary estates make for a rare tranquillity. Note especially the Baroque masterpiece Tserkov Klimenta (Church of St Clement, to the right down Klimentovskiy Pereulok) and Tserkov Vsyekh Skorbyashikh Radosty (Church of the Joy of All who Sorrow). *Cut down Chernigovskiy Pereulok to reach Pyatnitskaya Ulitsa.*

6 To the Kremlin

On the right you come to the small stone Tserkov Chernigovskikh Chudotvortsev (Church of the Chernigov Miracle Workers), and to the left Tserkov Ioana (Church of St John). Turning left on to well-preserved Pyatnitskaya Ulitsa, note on the right-hand corner the restored headquarters of the original Smirnoff vodka company. *Cross the bridge, continuing to the Kremlin.*

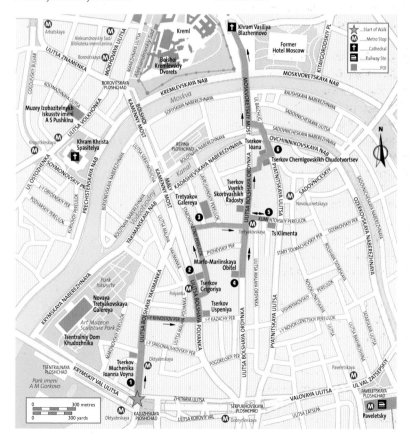

Tretyakovskaya Galereya (Tretyakov Gallery)

The Tretyakov Gallery boasts the largest collection of Russian art in the world (some 100,000 paintings in all). It was founded by the millionaire industrialist Pavel Tretyakov, who presented his private collection to the city of Moscow in 1892. The original building was designed in the Russian revivalist style by Viktor Vasnetsov and completed in 1905.

The gallery was closed in 1985 for a comprehensive programme of restoration completed in the 1990s. There is a second picture gallery, the Novaya Tretyakovskaya Galereya (known familiarly as the Tretyakovka), devoted to 20th-century art. This is on a different site entirely.

Old site *(Tretyakov) Lavrushinskiy Pereulok 12. Tel: 495 951 1362. www.tretyakov.ru. Open: Tue–Sun 10am–7pm (last admissions 6.30pm). Admission charge. Tours available in English. Metro: Tretyakovskaya.*

New site *(Tretyakovka) Krymskiy Val Ulitsa 10/14. Tel: 499 238 1378. Open: Tue–Sun 10am–7.30pm (last admissions 6.30pm). Admission charge. Tours available in English. Metro: Park Kultury.*

Icon painting

Icon painting, like Christianity itself, came to Russia via Byzantium. Most of the earliest icons are from Kiev, the cradle of Russian civilisation; the oldest, the austere Virgin of Vladimir, located in a church incorporated into the gallery's southern wing, dates from the 11th century. The early schools of Kiev, Novgorod and Pskov paved the way for artists of the naturalistic Moscow school, which flourished from the 14th to 17th centuries. There are masterpieces by the great trio of Moscow iconographers – Theophanes the Greek, Dionysius and Andrey Rublyov, as well as the 17th-century master Simon Ushakov.

18th- and 19th-century art

The story of Russian art continues on the second floor with the European-trained painters of the Academy of Arts, founded by Catherine the Great in the 18th century. The works on show include portraits and landscapes by Dmitry Levitsky, Vladimir Borovikovskiy and Vasily Tropinin.

In the 1870s a group of artists including Ivan Kramskoi, Vasily Perov and Fedor Vasilev rebelled against the straitjacket of academicism and went in search of a new, national art. The subject matter of these artists, who became known as the *Peredvizhniki* (the Wanderers) and went on to include Vasily Surikov, Vasily Polenov, Alexey Sarasov and the prolific Ilya Repin, ranges from portraits and vast historical canvases, through landscapes and religious paintings to vivid exposés of the horrors of war and the causes of social conflict (*see also pp68–9*).

After the Wanderers

Within the space of a generation, the Wanderers had been overtaken by a new wave of artists including several future collaborators of Diaghilev's Ballets Russes: Valentin Serov, Alexander Benois and Konstantin Korovin.

In the 20th century Russian painters entered the vanguard of European art, with Mikhail Larionov, Natalya Goncharova and Kazimir Malevich. Their work is highly original, but there is clear evidence too of the influence of the European Cubo-Futurist school. Many of these artists, including Vasily Kandinsky, were forced to leave Russia after the Revolution because of tightening ideological constraints.

The New Tretyakov

The New Tretyakov Gallery takes over where the old one left off with artists of the early 20th century. Most of the Soviet art belongs to the Socialist Realist school, which set out in the 1920s as an attempt to make art more accessible to the people, but which later degenerated into an ideological tool of the regime. What's on offer is a movable feast, but some of the more original artists to look out for include Isaak Brodsky, Alexander Deyneka and Sergei Gerasimov. The second floor holds temporary exhibitions by contemporary artists (*separate charge*).

The New Tretyakov Gallery on Krymskiy Val Ulitsa

Lenin, yesterday's hero

Muzey Istorii Goroda Moskvy (Museum of the History of Moscow)

The systematic destruction of religion in the capital is but one of the themes illustrated by this collection of prints, lithographs and archaeological bits and pieces relating to Moscow's chequered history and occupying the former Church of St John the Evangelist.
Novaya Ploshchad 12. Tel: 495 624 8490. www.mosmuseum.ru. Open: Tue–Sun 11am–5.30pm. Admission charge. Metro: Lubyanka.

Novaya Tretyakovskaya Galereya (New Tretyakov Gallery)

The back half of the Central Artists' House (*see p57*) hosts temporary exhibitions from the collections of the Tretyakov Gallery. Its main exhibition centres on 20th-century Russian art.
Tel: 499 238 1378. Open: Tue–Sun 10am–6.30pm.

Park imeni A M Gorkovo (Gorky Park)

Gorky Park stands on the banks of the Moskva River. You can stroll through this large park, or simply relax on numerous benches. Children enjoy the many rides in the local amusement park, but Gorky Park is certainly not just for children. It is a venue for regular concerts and many student celebrations.
Open: daily summer 10am–10pm; winter 10am–9pm. Admission charge. Cross the bridge approach road (Krymskiy Val) and follow the small street opposite.

Ploshchad Revolyutsii (Revolution Square)

Remains of the 16th-century city walls back the square, a favourite site of communist demonstrations to this day. Behind the walls is the cupola of the Zaikonospasskiy Monastery (*see p42*).

The ornate red-brick City Duma (council) building, on the left as you leave the metro, was the grandest of the USSR's Lenin museums, exhibiting his works in well over 100 languages.
Metro: Ploshchad Revolyutsii.

Traurny Poezd Lenina (Lenin's Funeral Train)

The train that transported Lenin's body from his country estate Gorki (*see pp86–7*), after his death on 21 January 1924, is displayed in a large pavilion beside the Paveletsky railway station. An inscription outside claims that, though Lenin is dead, his memory will live forever, as will his ideas and actions. If the pavilion is closed (as it often is), the train can still be seen through the glass windows.

Paveletsky Ploshchad 1. Open: Mon–Fri (officially) 10am–6pm. Free admission. Metro: Paveletskaya.

Tretyakovskaya Galereya (Tretyakov Gallery)

(*See pp54–5.*)

Tsentralniy Dom Khudozhnika (Central Artists' House)

This is Russia's premier exhibition centre of contemporary art. The gallery grounds are now home to many of Moscow's revolutionary statues: a kind of communist elephants' graveyard. The Central Artists' House was built in the 1970s for an exhibition of Soviet art. This project did not materialise and the building became the Central Artists' House instead. Part of it houses a branch of the Tretyakov Gallery with a permanent exhibition of 'Art of the 20th Century' (*see pp55–6*).

Krymskiy Val 10. Tel: 499 238 9843. www.cha.ru. Open: Tue–Sun 11am–8pm. Admission charge. Metro: Park Kultury.

Art Muzeon Sculpture Park

The grounds of the Central Artists' House became a resting place for many colossal statues of communist politicians and artists. After the fall of the regime, their prominent display on pedestals no longer seemed

The elegant façade of the Cathedral of the Epiphany

appropriate. It is quite odd to walk through this pleasant park looking at figures who were once among the most powerful in the world. Arts Park is also a good place to buy paintings.

EAST OF RED SQUARE
Bogoyavlenskiy Sobor v Yelokhove (Cathedral of the Epiphany at Yelokhov)

By legend the birthplace of the holy fool St Basil, the cathedral (originally built in the 13th century, completed in 1845) is among Moscow's most revered, serving as the patriarch's headquarters after his ejection by the communists from the Kremlin in 1918. The atmosphere of the resplendent interior during an evening service is unforgettable.

Spartakovskaya Ulitsa 15. Metro: Baumanskaya.

Botanicheskiy Sad (Botanical Gardens)

A wonderfully verdant retreat from Moscow's roaring boulevards, the university-run botanical gardens have existed on this site since the early 18th century.

Prospekt Mira 26. Tel: 495 680 5880. Open: daily 10am–10pm. Admission charge. Metro: Prospekt Mira.

Dom-Muzey Khudozhnika V M Vasnetsova (Viktor Vasnetsov House Museum)

One of the leaders of the Wanderers' artistic movement at the turn of the last century, Vasnetsov (1848–1926) is still much loved for his nostalgic renditions of Russia's mythical past. The interiors are superb.

Vasnetsova Pereulok 12. Open: Wed–Sun 10am–5pm. Closed: last Thur of month. Admission charge. Metro: Sukharevskaya.

Galereya Guelman (Guelman Gallery)

Marat Guelman exhibits the cream of the capital's artists. See the informative website for the latest details on exhibitions and sales.

4th Syromyatnicheskiy Pereulok 1. Tel: 495 228 1159. www.guelman.ru. Open: Tue–Sun noon–8pm. Free admission. Metro: Kurskaya/Chkalovskaya.

Galereya Shishkin (Shishkin Gallery)

Leonid Shishkin has been collecting since 1989, specialising in Russian art of the 19th and early 20th centuries and post-war Soviet painting.

Neglinnaya Ulitsa 29. Tel: 495 694 3510. www.shishkin-gallery.ru. Open: Mon–Fri 11am–8pm, Sat noon–6pm. Free admission. Metro: Tsvetnoi Bulvar.

Komsomolskaya Ploshchad (Komsomol Square)

'Komsomol' was the abbreviation of the League of Young Communists, whose members helped build the palatial metro station beneath your feet.

Above ground, equally memorable is the architecture of the railway termini surrounding the square. Yaraslavlsky Vokzal (Yaroslavl Station), start of the grand Trans-Siberian railway (and adjoining the Leningrad terminus), was built in Russian fairytale style by Fyodor Shekhtel in 1902–4, while the exuberant Kazansky Vokzal (Kazan Station) is the work of Aleksey Shchusev, better known for designing Lenin's Mausoleum (*see p41*).

Between the stations stands the Leningrad Hotel, one of seven 'wedding cake' buildings constructed to Stalin's taste in the 1940s and 1950s.

Metro: Komsomolskaya.

Lubyanka (The Lubyanka)

Lenin established the KGB's forerunner – the CheKa – in the Rossiya Insurance building on Lubyanskaya Ploshchad. *Pravda* outlined his policy of terror in 1918: 'Do not demand incriminating evidence to prove that the prisoner has opposed the Soviet government …

How under the eyelids terror lurks,
How suffering inscribes on cheeks the
hard lines of its cuneiform texts ...' The
Lubyanka remained a symbol of
repression until 1991 when it was the
scene of demonstrations, culminating
in the toppling of the statue of CheKa
founder Felix Dzerzhinskiy – and
symbolically the Soviet regime. The
statue now graces the Art Muzeon
Sculpture Park (*see p57*) alongside
many others from the communist era.
Lubyanskaya Ploshchad.
Metro: Lubyanka.

Communists demonstrating outside the former KGB headquarters in Lubyanka Square

Your first duty is to ask him to which
class he belongs ... This question
should decide the fate of the prisoner.'

Successor organisations to the
CheKa, like the NKVD, became the
instrument of Stalin's crackdown on
real and imaginary Party opposition
in the 1930s. Many of the victims
disappeared through the back gates
of the dour Lubyanka building on
Furkasovskiy Pereulok: torture and
execution took place in the courtyard
and basement. Between five and seven
million were arrested in the Great
Purge of 1937–8 alone, most ending up
– and dying – in the Gulag Archipelago
of prison camps.

The poem *Requiem* by Anna
Akhmatova (1888–1966) vividly recalls
the systematic repression of the purges.
'I have learnt how faces fell to bone,

Lubyanka 12
(Security Service Museum)

Located in the old KGB social club, this
fascinating museum aims to polish the
tarnished image of the Russian security
services. The exhibits include CheKa
leader Felix Dzerzhinskiy's desk,
cameras and other spy paraphernalia,
revolvers and contraband seized by the
KGB's successor, the FSB.
Lubyanka 12. Open for guided tours only
by Patriarshy Dom Tours, tel: 795 0927.
Metro: Lubyanka.

Lubyanskaya Ploshchad
(Lubyanka Square)

The square is dominated by the
Lubyanka (*see above*), nickname of
the former KGB's headquarters. To the
right is the 19th-century Polytechnic
Museum building (*see p65*), while to
the left is Russia's biggest toyshop,
Detskiy Mir (Children's World).
Metro: Lubyanka.

Walk: Kuznetskiy Most and the Neglinnaya

A little of the 19th-century exclusivity of Kuznetskiy Most is being reborn in brightly lit shop windows, while the backstreets giving on to the Bulvar reach deep into Moscow's medieval past.

Allow 1¹/₂ hours, excluding visits to the steam baths and circus.

Head straight for Kuznetskiy Most from the metro station of the same name.

1 The Neglinnaya River

Kuznetskiy Most – Smiths' Bridge – is named after the metalworkers in the cannon foundry established on the left bank of the Neglinnaya River by Ivan the Terrible. Though the bridge was dismantled when the river was enclosed underground, its name lived on in the city's centre of finance and fashion. The jeweller Fabergé displayed his marvels in today's 'Rifle' clothing shop, while around the corner at Neglinnaya Ulitsa 12 stands the Central Bank of the Russian Federation.
Continue right along Neglinnaya Ulitsa, then turn right into Sandunovskiy Pereulok.

2 Sandunovskiye Banyi (Sandunov Baths)

Much loved by Moscow's literati – the author Chekhov had a private room overlooking No 2 – the historic steam baths at Sandunovskiy Pereulok 14 are worth a look. The interior, with its carved oak cubicles, stained glass and elegant light fittings dating from the early 19th century, breathes faded grandeur. (*For details on Russian banya procedures, see p158.*)
Turn left at the end of Sandunovskiy Pereulok on to Ulitsa Rozhdestvenka.

3 To Stretenskiy Monastyr

The 18th-century country house to the left with the prettily tiled façade is Moscow's Architectural Institute. Tserkov Nikolay v Zvonaryakh (Church of St Nicholas in Zvonaryakh) next door houses the institute's drawing school.

Turning right down Bolshoi Kiselniy Pereulok and left on to Ulitsa Lubyanka Bolshaya, you reach the remains of the Stretenskiy Monastery, founded in 1395. Built in honour of the miraculous icon that came to Tamerlane in a dream and dissuaded him from attacking Moscow, the cathedral and its glorious frescos are now under restoration following years of abuse when it was used as a club for members of the KGB. *Turn left onto Rozhdestvenskiy Bulvar.*

4 Rozhdestvenskiy Bulvar and Monastyr

The most elegant of the capital's boulevards begins with the tiny chapel of Our Lady Most Holy, attached to a derelict church. Opposite on Stretenskiy Bulvar a statue to Lenin's wife, Nadezhda Krupskaya, stands in place of the Stretenskiy Gates – pulled down by Stalin in the 1930s.

The far western corner of Rozhdestvenskiy Bulvar is the site of a convent, constructed in 1386. Although the convent was closed soon after the Revolution, two old nuns, Varvara and Viktorina, continued to live there until

the former was strangled by an icon-smuggler in 1978. The convent has now reopened.

Enjoy the view from the end of the boulevard and walk down to the square.

5 Trubnaya Ploshchad and Tsvetnoi Bulvar

Trubnaya Ploshchad used to be the site of livestock and bird markets. On Annunciation Day (25 March), Muscovites traditionally bought birds to release into the air – profitable business for the traders who trained them to return for subsequent resale. Neighbouring Tsvetnoi Bulvar was the city's main flower market but is now home to the *Tsirk* (State Circus – *see p157*).

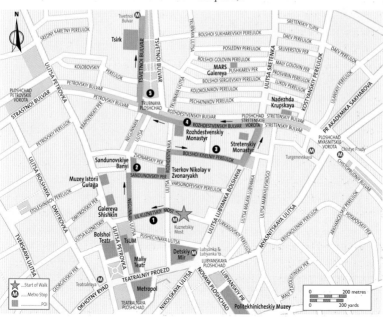

Drink and be merry

When thinking about Russia, one of the first things that comes to mind is vodka, the national drink. No celebration, party or even Sunday lunch is complete without it. Russian vodka is good and relatively cheap, but its popularity has caused much hardship among Russians over the years. The abuse of vodka still creates serious problems and even led to prohibition under Gorbachev.

But prohibition merely gave rise to an illicit trade in alcohol, while others turned to home-brewed *samogon*, which caused many deaths from alcohol poisoning. The ban on alcohol did not solve or improve anything. Fortunately, in recent years increasing numbers of Russians have started to turn away from hard liquor and lead a more healthy life, though consumption is still absurdly high.

Besides being *the* vodka country, Russia is becoming famous for its many kinds of beer (*pivo*). Their quality can easily compete with other

You can get *kvas* on tap in bars and at street kiosks throughout Moscow and St Petersburg

European brands. Russia's cheap labour force has attracted foreign breweries from the USA, the Netherlands and even South Africa. Every shop in Russia boasts at least 20 brands of Russian or foreign beer. In summer, restaurant gardens are packed with Muscovites enjoying their beer with the obligatory dried fish, called *vobla* or *taranka*. Some Russians even drink *yorsh* – a beer and vodka cocktail! By the way, it is quite normal in Russia to walk around the city while drinking beer straight from the bottle, though city authorities occasionally crack down on public drinking.

There are other characteristic drinks enjoyed by Russians that are alcohol-free. Tea is important in everyday life. 'Russian tea' is always drunk black and it is made with only a small amount of water, so it is very strong. This potent extract is poured into individual tea cups and each drinker dilutes it to taste with boiling water. Traditionally sugar is not placed in the tea, but either bitten off a large sugar lump, or placed in the mouth and the tea drunk through it (though you're unlikely to ever see anyone actually doing this). While enjoying their tea, Russians like to munch on something, such as red or black caviar on bread and butter – or chocolate.

Another favourite drink is *kvas*, which is a bread-based, sweet

A Russian samovar

beverage – rather like beer, but only mildly alcoholic. It is quite filling and Russians drink it with *pirozhki* (savoury doughnuts) or *blini* (pancakes). *Pirozhki* are filled with mince, mushroom, cabbage or a fruit marmalade. They really match the sweet and slightly heavy taste of *kvas*.

Russians are very hospitable, so if you are ever invited to a Russian home, be prepared: you will be expected to eat and drink large quantities. The unprepared stomach may suffer from overload and nothing calms it better than the typical Russian sour milk called *kefir*.

MARS Galereya (MARS Gallery)

This gallery in a northeastern suburb is one of Moscow's foremost exhibition centres of contemporary works. The founders were among those whose exhibitions were bulldozed by the authorities in the 1970s. Not all works here are of the highest quality, but all are interesting and inspiring. Work is regularly on sale and credit cards are accepted.

Pushkaryov Pereulok 5. Tel: 495 623 5610. www.marsgallery.ru. Open: Tue–Sun noon–8pm. Free admission. Metro: Tsvetnoi Bulvar.

Muzey Andreya Sakharova (Sakharov Museum)

Nuclear physicist and Nobel Peace Prize laureate Andrei Sakharov was a vocal opponent of the Soviet system and this museum contains exhibitions about his life, the Gulag and human rights.

Zemlyanoy Val 57. Tel: 495 623 4401. www.sakharov-center.ru. Open: Tue–Sun 11am–7pm. Free admission. Metro: Chkalovskaya.

Muzey Drevnerusskoi Kultury i Iskusstva imeni Andreya Rublyova (Rublyov Museum of Ancient Russian Culture and Art)

You will find a rich display of religious art on show in the Andronnikov Monastery and can also visit the museum's adjoining restoration studios.

Andronyevskaya Ploshchad 10. Tel: 495 678 1467. Open: Thur–Tue 11am–5pm. Closed: last Fri of month. Admission charge. Metro: Ploshchad Ilyicha.

Novospasskiy Monastyr (New Monastery of the Saviour)

This pretty monastery (1490), on a lakeside hill by the Moskva River, has a sinister past. It has been a children's

The Polytechnic Museum has displays showcasing various spheres of technology

prison, a sobering-up centre for arrested female drunks, and a base of the NKVD secret police, forerunner of the KGB. Summary executions were carried out in the monastery grounds – mass graves of the victims were discovered in the banks beneath the monastery towers after the complex was surrendered to the church in 1991.

The central Cathedral of the Transfiguration (1647), built as the family church of the Romanov dynasty, now holds services again.
Krestyanskaya Ploshchad 10.
Tel: 495 676 9570.
Open: daily 7am–7pm.
Metro: Krestyanskaya Zastava.

Politekhinicheskiy Muzey (Polytechnic Museum)

A little rusted and loose at the seams, the displays on the achievements of Soviet science and industry are still worth a visit. Some exhibits are labelled in English. There are many models of mining, nuclear and other machinery. It is a must for all interested in science, chemistry or technology.
Novaya Ploshchad 3/4.
Tel: 495 623 0756. Open: Tue–Sun 10am–5pm. Closed: last Thur of month. Admission charge. Metro: Lubyanka/Kitay-Gorod.

Staraya Ploshchad (Old Square)

A thriving marketplace in the 19th century, Staraya Ploshchad was better known more recently as the home of the Communist Party Central Committee (building No 4), ideological epicentre of the Soviet Union. Some of the area's old charm is captured in the 1694 Tserkov Vsyekh Svyatikh (Church of All Saints) at the far end of the square and the gloriously decorated Church of the Trinity on nearby Nikitnikov Pereulok (*see p43*).
Metro: Kitay-Gorod.

Taganskaya Ploshchad (Taganka Square)

Much of the 19th-century anthill of artisans' dwellings, cheap hostels and taverns in this quarter was destroyed by Soviet town planners, leaving little more than a vast expanse. However, it was celebrated under communism for the barely tolerated Taganka Theatre and its favourite son, Russia's Bob Dylan, Vladimir Vysotsky, who died of drink in 1980.
Metro: Taganskaya.

Winzavod

Five fascinating galleries now fill a recently renovated wine-bottling factory near the Kursky railway station. The work on display is pretty cutting-edge and you'll have to dig very deep if you're in the market to make a purchase!
Siromyatnicheskiy Pereulok 1.
Tel: 495 917 4646. www.winzavod.ru.
Open: Tue–Sun noon–8pm.
Free admission.
Metro: Chkalovskaya.

WEST OF RED SQUARE
A-3 Galereya (A-3 Gallery)

One of Moscow's best, this gallery is at the forefront of the city's modern art scene.

Starokonyushenniy Pereulok 39.
Tel: 495 691 8484.
Open: Wed–Sun 11am–7pm.
Free admission. Metro: Smolenskaya.

Beliy Dom (White House)

Gleaming on the banks of the river opposite the Stalinist skyscraper Ukraine Hotel, the White House once stood at the heart of the battle for Russia's political future. As the House of Soviets of the Russian Federation, it was the site of makeshift barricades against the abortive 1991 coup, when crowds swamped half-hearted tank commanders sent in to restore order.

In October 1993, this time as the Russian Parliament, the building was the focus of hostilities between President Yeltsin and hardline deputies.

The White House, home to the Russian Parliament

It looked, briefly, as though the communists were triumphant until Yeltsin ordered tanks to bombard the building into submission: 138 people were killed. Repairs cost over $80 million (£48 million).

The now gleaming, but heavily fenced-off building is home to Prime Minister Putin's office and staff, as well as the Russian government's official offices.

Konyushkovskaya Ulitsa. Metro: Krasnopresnenskaya.

Dom-Muzey i Literaturniy Muzey A S Pushkina (Alexander Pushkin Literature Museum)

The reverence reserved for Russia's premier poet (1799–1837) far exceeds that of the English for Shakespeare and the Germans for Goethe. It is evidenced in the hushed awe with which local visitors pore over the author's collected manuscripts, jottings and possessions gathered in two museums, the second of which was Pushkin's home for a short time.

Literaturniy Muzey A S Pushkina, Ulitsa Prechistenka 12. Tel: 495 637 5674. Open: Tue–Sun 10am–5pm. Closed: last Fri of month. Admission charge. Metro: Kropotkinskaya. Dom-Muzey A S Pushkina, Arbat 53. Tel: 499 241 9293. Open: Wed–Sun 10am–5pm. Closed: last Fri of month. Admission charge. Metro: Smolenskaya.

Khram Pokrova na Filyakh (Church of the Intercession at Fili)

Although for long not a working church, this is well worth a visit as one of the most striking examples of Muscovite High Baroque architecture. Icons from the Rublyov Museum of Ancient Russian Culture and Art are on permanent display within.

Novozavodskaya Ulitsa, 10 minutes' walk north from Fili Metro. Tel: 495 148 4552. Open: Wed–Mon 11am–5pm. Closed: first Fri of month. Admission charge.

Khram Simeona Stolpnika (Church of St Simon Stylites)

It is the juxtaposition of this little church against the monolithic tower blocks of the Novy Arbat that makes the building – bare inside after years of service as the All-Russia Nature Conservancy Society exhibition hall – a photographic favourite. Built in 1649, the church had its moment of glory with the wedding in 1801 of the fabulously rich Count Sheremetev to one of his serfs.

Ulitsa Povarskaya 5. Tel: 495 291 2184. Metro: Arbatskaya.

Muzey Dekorativno-Prikladnovo Iskusstva (Applied Arts Museum)

A stunning exhibition of traditional arts including jewellery, ceramics and superb lacquered boxes.

Ulitsa Delegatskaya 3. Tel: 495 623 7725. Open: Sat–Thur 10am–5pm. Closed: last Thur of month. Admission charge. Metro: Tsvetnoi Bulvar.

Muzey Istorii Gulaga (Gulag Museum)

A memorial to the victims of the Gulag system, this museum looks at the prison camps and the life of those who were sent there for the slightest misdemeanour, criticism of the state or even cracking a joke about Stalin in the wrong company.

Ulitsa Petrovka 16. Tel: 495 621 7346. Open: Tue–Sat 11am–4pm. Admission charge. Metro: Chekhovskaya.

Muzey Izobrazitelnykh Iskusstv imeni A S Pushkina (Pushkin Fine Arts Museum)

While the Pushkin Museum has good collections of classical and Egyptian antiquities and copies of Renaissance sculpture, it is best known for its rich holdings of European painting – especially the French Impressionists. The upper floor has important works by Cézanne, Manet, Monet, Gauguin, Matisse and Picasso (rooms 17–18 and

(*Cont. on p74*)

The artistic explosion

In the late 19th and early 20th centuries, Russia was gripped by a momentous revolution in the arts that paralleled the turbulent atmosphere of the times. The spirit was one of experiment, a true *fin de siècle* rejection of outmoded doctrines and dusty prejudices.

In 1863, exasperated by its enforced adherence to classical subjects, 14 artists walked out of the St Petersburg Academy of Arts and formed their own group, known as the *Peredvizhniki* (the Wanderers) for their travelling exhibitions. Their work dealt innovatively with social issues, epitomised by the searching pictorial parables of Ilya Repin.

Artists were now being supported by Russia's growing class of businessmen, like the railway magnate Savva Mamontov (*see p86*) and the merchant Pavel Tretyakov, whose collection of Russian art forms the heart of the Tretyakov Gallery (*see pp54–5*).

The 'World of Art' – *Mir Iskusstva* – movement at the turn of the 20th century was driven by the impresario Sergei Diaghilev, whose aim was to 'exalt Russian art in the eyes of the West'. Members such as Alexander Benois, Leon Bakst and Valentin Serov not only galvanised Russian Impressionism and art nouveau, but also designed sets and costumes for Diaghilev, whose Ballets Russes took Europe by storm. The inspired choreography of Michel Fokine and breathtaking dancing of Anna Pavlova and Vaslav Nijinsky, combined with the extraordinary scores of Igor Stravinsky's *Firebird* and *Rite of Spring*, revolutionised ballet.

The Tretyakov Gallery is known for its valuable exhibits

Inside the Bolshoi Theatre, Moscow

The Moscow Art Theatre sprang to prominence with the plays of Anton Chekhov and their interpretation by Konstantin Stanislavsky, whose concentration on naturalness gained worldwide renown as the Stanislavsky Method.

Over the years surrounding the 1917 Revolution, Russian artists, such as Mikhail Larionov, Natalya Goncharova and Kazimir Malevich, were the undisputed leaders of the avant-garde. Movements mushroomed: Primitivism, Rayonnism, Futurism, Supremacism, Constructivism …

The poet of the Revolution, Vladimir Mayakovsky, declared: 'We do not need a dead mausoleum of art where dead works are worshipped, but a living factory of the human spirit.' His contemporaries followed his lead, committing themselves wholeheartedly to the great communist experiment which, by the 1930s, had silenced them all.

Walk: The Arbat

Dirty-kneed children and frock-coated merchants ... the last decades of a doomed aristocracy ... underground printing presses and impoverished artists ... this is the soul of the Arbat quarter of the city that still filters through today's pedestrian mall and souvenir shops. The grimy courtyards and twisting backstreets readily conjure up scenes of working-class life at the inception of the Revolution, while the time-worn mansions of Ulitsa Prechistenka speak of an age never to return.

Allow 2¹/2 hours. Start at Arbatskaya metro. Take a look at the vast Ministry of Defence (Ministerstvo Oboroniy) building behind you before crossing the road to Ulitsa Arbat.

1 Ulitsa Arbat

Alive with street musicians, beggars, snappily dressed mafiosi and long-haired youths, the Arbat retains something of the bohemian atmosphere of days gone by.

This area played host at various times to such luminaries as writers Pushkin, Lermontov, Tolstoy, Gogol and Bulgakov and composers Scriabin and Rachmaninov. The street was also a hotbed of political dissent – No 9 housed one of the country's largest anti-tsarist printing presses.

Once the main route to Russia's western lands, the Arbat was the road to Stalin's dacha in the 1930s, patrolled by a legion of secret police for whom the luxurious Praga restaurant (on the right-hand corner) was converted into

a dining hall. The concentration of intelligentsia made the area a prime target of Stalin's terror, as recorded in Anatoly Rybakov's novel *Children of the Arbat* – hugely popular during the *glasnost* era. The author lived at No 51.

Make a detour left down Bolshaya Afanasevskiy Pereulok, turn left and then right on to Filippovskiy Pereulok.

2 Side streets

As you make your way along the Arbat, duck into as many of the courtyards and side streets as you can. Heading down Krivoarbatskiy Pereulok, No 10 was the home of the modernist architect Konstantin Melnikov, dubbed 'the Russian Le Corbusier', whose genius was ultimately snuffed out by Stalin – for 40 years not one of

Note: Large parts of the Arbat are under reconstruction. Works move from building to building; it is therefore difficult to say which will be next.

Melnikov's projects was realised. To the right up Spasopeskovskiy Pereulok is the residence of US Ambassadors to Russia, Spaso House, built in 1914. Spasopeskovskaya Ploshchadka 36, where Scriabin used to give concerts, is a wonderful example of the Russian carved *izba* (wooden cottage). Return to Ulitsa Arbat, then go left down Plotnikov Pereulok.

Wander south between the embassies in one of the city's most fashionable residential districts until you come to Ulitsa Prechistenka, the aristocratic stronghold of old Moscow. No 12 is now Literaturniy Muzey A S Pushkina, a museum devoted to the poet Pushkin, while No 11, Muzey

L N Tolstovo, is dedicated to Tolstoy (*see pp74–5*).

3 Khram Khrista Spasitelya

Until 1934, the vast Cathedral of Christ the Saviour dominated the city skyline. It was blown up to make way for what was to have been the world's largest building, Stalin's Palace of the Soviets. Khrushchev abandoned the project and work began on a replica of the old cathedral. It was consecrated in 1999 (*see pp44–5*). The cathedral also contains a museum.

Muzey Khrama Khrista Spasitelya, Ulitsa Volkhonka 15. Tel: 495 924 8058. Open: daily 10am–6pm. Free admission. Metro: Kropotkinskaya.

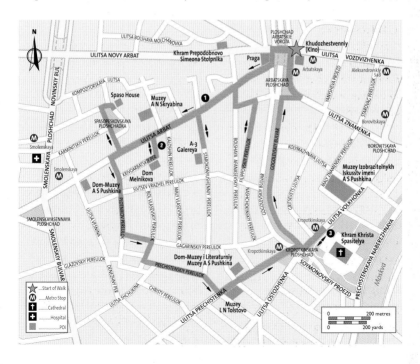

Walk: Tverskaya Ulitsa and Patriarshiy Prud

Named after the market town of Tver, 150km (93 miles) north of Moscow, Tverskaya Ulitsa's broad expanse begins the long highway to St Petersburg. It was reconstructed as Gorky Street in the 1930s to Stalin's grandiose taste. The upmarket shops demonstrate the new-found wealth of many Muscovites; the contrastingly peaceful environs are the focus of much of the capital's literary history.

Allow 2½ hours. Begin at Mayakovskaya metro station.

1 Triumfalnaya Ploshchad (Square of Triumph)

'Comrades, to the barricades! ... Streets are our brushes, squares are our palettes!' Thus exhorted the poet Vladimir Mayakovsky, the laureate of Soviet communism, whose statue dominates the square. Behind him stands the Stalinist Peking Hotel, while to his right are the Tchaikovsky Concert Hall and Theatre of Satire.
Walk down Tverskaya Ulitsa towards the Kremlin.

2 Muzey Sovremennoi Istorii Rossii (Museum of Contemporary History)

(*See p75.*)

3 Pushkinskaya Ploshchad (Pushkin Square)

In summer amorous couples and drunks compete for benches in the shade around the statue of Russia's national poet, Alexander Pushkin. For centuries a favourite meeting place, it is now the site of the world's largest McDonald's restaurant.
Continue down the left of the street.

4 Lower Tverskaya Ulitsa

Passing the waxworks museum at No 14 (*see p156*), the faded glory of the adjoining Yeliseev's food store is worth a look before reaching Tverskaya Ploshchad, where Moscow's founder, Yuri Dolgorukiy, faces the city council building. A world-weary Lenin sits in isolation to his rear, oblivious of the reconstruction to his left of 18th-century Tserkov Cosmy i Damiana (Church of Sts Cosmo and Damian). The façades of Nos 9 and 11 across the road are built of granite earmarked by the Germans for a victory monument following the expected fall of Moscow. Through the arch gleams the cupola of the 17th-century Tserkov Vozneseniya (Church of the Ascension).

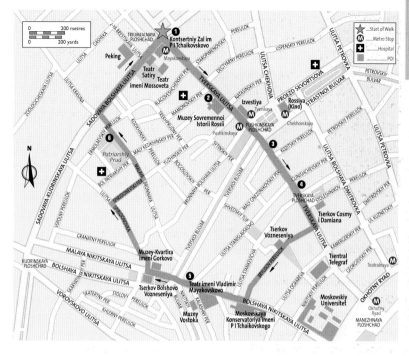

Turn into Bryusov Pereulok and then right again into Bolshaya Nikitskaya Ulitsa and away from the centre.

5 Literary Moscow

The TASS news agency stands at the corner of Bolshaya Nikitskaya Ulitsa and the Bulvar. Author Maxim Gorky is remembered in the art nouveau house-museum (Muzey-Kvartira imeni Gorkovo) at nearby Malaya Nikitskaya Ulitsa 6/2 (*see p74*). Next comes the house of poet Alexander Blok; opposite lived the writer Alexey Tolstoy, a distant relative of *the* Tolstoy.

Turn right on Ulitsa Spiridonovka, then right along Spiridonevski Pereulok, then left on to Malaya Bronnaya Ulitsa.

6 Bulgakov's Moscow

When the Devil comes to torment Moscow in Mikhail Bulgakov's masterpiece *The Master and Margarita*, he makes his first appearance at the tranquil Patriarshiy Prud (Patriarch's Ponds). The novel was suppressed by Stalin and was not published until 1966. Its author died blind and penniless in 1940. Much of the action is set around the corner in apartment 50, Sadovaya Bolshaya Ulitsa 10, where Bulgakov lived in the early 1920s. The graffiti festooning the staircase bear witness to the cult-like following he enjoys to this day.

Turn right on to Sadovaya Bolshaya Ulitsa to return to Mayakovskaya.

The impressive Pushkin Fine Arts Museum

21). Earlier European artists, including Rembrandt, Rubens, El Greco and Botticelli, are well represented.

The museum rocked the art world in 1995 when it showed for the first time paintings plundered from private collections by Soviet troops at the end of World War II, including *Carnival* by Goya, Manet's *Portrait of Rosita Maury*, El Greco's *St Bernard*, and *Portrait of Madame Choquet at the Window* by Renoir. Many had been written off as lost masterpieces. Whether the paintings will remain in the museum is a matter of diplomatic debate: the ambassador of Germany, from where most of the works were taken, first knew of their existence when he received an invitation to the exhibition's opening day, and the embassy has since demanded their return.
Ulitsa Volkhonka 12. Tel: 495 203 7998. www.museum.ru/gmii. Open: Tue–Sun 10am–6pm. Admission charge. Tours in English and audio-guides are available. Metro: Kropotkinskaya.

Muzey-Kvartira imeni Gorkovo (Maxim Gorky House Museum)

Despite his serious misgivings about the 1917 Revolutions, Gorky (1868–1936) was lionised by the state as a pillar of proletarian literature and promoted as a model for young Soviet writers. Coaxed back from emigration and disillusion in 1928, Gorky lived in a wonderful example of Russian avant-garde architecture till his death, rumoured to be at Stalin's prompting.
*Malaya Nikitskaya Ulitsa 6/2. Tel: 495 690 5130. Open: Wed–Sun 11am–6pm. Free admission.
Metro: Arbatskaya/Pushkinskaya.*

Muzey L N Tolstovo (Lev Tolstoy House Museum)

The grand old man of Russian literature (1828–1910) is remembered in two Moscow museums. Despite Tolstoy's espousal in later life of such doctrines as vegetarianism and pacifism, his stature was such that even the strict censors of communist aesthetics were forced to leave his works and memory untouched. The Muzey-Usadba Lva Tolstovo, the house where Tolstoy lived between 1882 and 1901, is especially evocative and a must-see.
Ulitsa Prechistenka 11. Tel: 495 637 7410. Open: Tue–Sun 11am–6pm. Closed: last Fri of month. Admission charge. Metro: Kropotkinskaya.

Muzey-Usadba Lva Tolstovo, Ulitsa Lva Tolstovo 21. Tel: 499 246 9444. Open: Wed–Sun 10am–5pm. Admission charge. Metro: Park Kultury.

Muzey Sovremennoi Istorii Rossii (Museum of Contemporary History)

Rather than close down what was once a centrepiece of tourist-orientated propaganda, the curators have produced an even-handed tour through the convulsions of Russia's revolutionary past. The exhibits range from bold communist posters to a tableau of the barricades of 1991 as the Soviet Union drew its final gasps for survival.

The crumpled trolleybus in the forecourt found itself in the path of a tank during the abortive 1991 coup.
Tverskaya Ulitsa 21. Tel: 495 299 5217/ 6724. Open: Tue–Sat 10am–6pm, Sun 10am–5pm. Closed: last Fri of month. Admission charge. Metro: Tverskaya.

Gorky's art nouveau house

Muzey Vostoka (Museum of the East)

In a building dating from 1821, this museum takes us for a trip to the East, each country distinguished by a different-coloured background. Archaeological discoveries from the Caucasus and Asia are displayed alongside presents from China, North Korea and Iran. Almost impossible to describe, the displays are as colourful and as diverse as the cultures themselves.
Nikitskiy Bulvar 12a. Tel: 495 202 4555. Open: Tue–Sun 11am–8pm. Admission charge. Metro: Arbatskaya.

Pushkinskaya Ploshchad (Pushkin Square)

The elegant Strastnoy Monastery was torn down in 1937 to make room for this favourite Moscow meeting place at the intersection of Tverskaya Ulitsa and the Bulvar (*see p72*). The monument to Pushkin, unveiled in 1880 in the presence of writers Ivan Turgenev and Fyodor Dostoevsky, is on the western side of the square.
Metro: Pushkinskaya/Tverskaya.

Teatralnaya Ploshchad (Theatre Square)

The Bolshoi (Big) Theatre, designed in 1825 by Osip Bove, is both an architectural and a cultural Moscow landmark. Rivalled only by St Petersburg's Mariinskiy (formerly Kirov) Theatre, its stage has played host (*Cont. on p78*)

Stalin's skyscrapers

Any visitor to Moscow will soon encounter a monumental, neoclassicist high-rise building, with the Soviet emblem and maybe a star on its beacon. After a day or two in Moscow, one finds this building seems to dominate the city.

At this point, do not make the usual tourist mistake. Never use this building as a landmark: there are seven of them and they are almost identical!

Known as Stalin's skyscrapers, they were built in the 1940s and 1950s at the dictator's behest. Meant to commemorate 800 years of Moscow's history, in fact they represent the might of the Soviet Union in the 1950s, when it was perhaps the most powerful country in the world. The Soviet 'empire', including many satellite states, reached from the Pacific in the East to the Baltic Sea in the West. It was exporting the communist ideology across the world and the USSR was gaining the upper hand in the arms and space races with the USA.

Two of these skyscrapers serve as ordinary apartment blocks, though they are anything but ordinary. They are in the city centre and the apartments are very large, so they are only for the very well-off. Visitors can sample these buildings by checking in to the Hotel Ukraine (currently closed for renovation) or Hotel Leningrad (now the Hilton) (see Accommodation pp172–7), the third and fourth of the series. Two more house the Ministry of Interior and the Ministry of Transport and Services, but the one that is really worth visiting is the State Lomonosov University, in Sparrow (formerly Lenin) Hills, a favourite destination for newlyweds and tourists alike. A large fountain right in front of the building emphasises its monumental size.

The construction of these buildings was under the direct supervision of one of Stalin's most notorious henchmen – Lavrenty Beria, who led the feared NKVD (later KGB). In 1993, during reconstruction of his former villa, dozens of skeletons were found in his garden. He was executed soon after Stalin's death.

If the weather allows, there is a beautiful view from the university over a very large part of Moscow, from an unusual perspective. The view is dominated by the large Luzhniki Stadium, built for the 1980 Olympic Games, which were boycotted by the USA. Four years later there was no Soviet team at the Olympics held in Los Angeles.

Although these buildings contain no tourist attraction, they inspire deep nostalgia among Muscovites for the once mighty and undefeated Soviet Union, where progress was the key word. If there are three things characteristic of Moscow, they are the Kremlin, Red Square and Stalin's skyscrapers. And if you happen to visit any former communist-bloc capital such as Riga, Warsaw or Prague, do not be surprised if you see one of them there too – a present from Soviet Russia.

One of the seven Stalinist skyscrapers

Exterior decoration on the Church of
St Nicholas of the Weavers

to attractions as diverse as the great
singer Fyodor Chaliapin and the 1922
founding ceremony of the Soviet Union
(*see also pp152–3*). It shares the square
with the Children's Theatre and the
Maliy (Small) Theatre, to its right and
left respectively. A huge granite
impression of Karl Marx looks across
Teatralniy Proezd.

A ceramic frieze enlivens the outside
of the luxuriously restored Metropol
Hotel (one of the oldest hotels in
Russia, designed in 1898 by William
Walcott) to Marx's right on Teatralniy
Proezd. Constructed at the turn of the
last century, its *style moderne* interior is
well worth a look.
Metro: Teatralnaya/Okhotny Ryad.

Tserkov Bolshovo Vozneseniya (Church of the Grand Ascension)

This monumental church witnessed the
wedding of Alexander Pushkin in 1831

and was loved by Tchaikovsky for its
marvellous acoustics. The Soviets
vandalised it thoroughly, converting it
by turn into a workshop, garage and
lightning conductor research laboratory.
Ulitsa Bolshaya Nikitskaya 36.
Metro: Arbatskaya.

Tserkov Nikoly v Khamovnikakh (Church of St Nicholas of the Weavers)

One of Moscow's best-loved – and
gaudiest – churches, St Nicholas dates
from the 17th century, when it was
commissioned by the city's weavers.
As eye-catching as the exterior is the
decoration inside – preserved because
the church remained open during
Soviet rule.
Ulitsa Lva Tolstovo 2.
Metro: Park Kultury.

OUTSIDE OF THE CENTRE
Danilovskiy Monastyr (Danilov Monastery)

Moscow's most ancient monastery
dates from 1282 and is named after its
founder, Prince Daniel, son of
Alexander Nevskiy. After use as a
juvenile delinquents' prison, it resumed
its role as the headquarters of the
Orthodox Patriarchate in 1988 (hence
its spruce appearance). The oldest
church within is the 17th-century
Church of the Holy Fathers, containing
Daniel's relics, and packed with
worshippers on church festivals.
Beggars throng the Church of Simeon
Stylites at the monastery entrance –

giving to the poor is a central element of the Orthodox faith, which is observed punctiliously today.

Entrance is free but, as in all Russian religious buildings, modest dress and respectful behaviour are expected.
Danilovskiy Val 22. Tel: 495 955 6757.
Open: daily 7am–7pm.
Metro: Tulskaya.

Galereya Russkoi Ledovoi Sculptury (Ice Sculpture Gallery)

An ice sculpture gallery is a winter thing, right? Wrong. The first year-round display of ice art is housed in a giant freezer kept at −10°C (14°C). Special clothing is dispensed to all visitors to keep them warm.
Krasnaya Presnya Park.
Tel: 495 220 4619.
Open: daily 11am–8pm.
Admission charge.
Metro: Ulitsa 1905 Goda.

Khram Rozhdestva Bogoroditsiy (Church of the Nativity of the Virgin)

This tiny church was once part of the neighbouring Simonov monastery erected by Russia's patron saint, Sergei Radonezhskiy. When the monastery was part-levelled to make way for the vast Zil works, the church was somehow left in the middle of the factory grounds. It is one of Moscow's most ancient churches, dating from 1509.
Ulitsa Vostochnaya 6.
Tel: 495 275 7011.
Metro: Avtozavodskaya.

Memorialniy Muzey Kosmonavtiki (Space Travel Museum)

Situated beneath the massive titanium rocket monument at VVTs, this museum contains a modest collection of space hardware ranging from early satellites to the spacesuits of the first cosmonaut, Yuri Gagarin, and a number of the dogs (now stuffed) blasted into orbit prior to Gagarin's flight.
Prospekt Mira 111. Tel: 495 683 8197.
Open: Tue–Sun 10am–7pm.
Closed: last Fri of month.
Admission charge.
Metro: VDNKh.

Novodevichiy Monastyr (New Convent of the Maidens)

Peter the Great banished his sister Sophia to a cell in this breathtakingly beautiful ensemble, for alleged participation in a revolt. The Austrian ambassador watched in horror as the culprits were tortured and hanged before her window: 'Nobody will easily believe how lamentable were their cries and howls, unless he has well weighed their excruciations and the greatness of their tortures.'

The convent's most notable buildings are the red-brick bell tower (1690) and the central Smolensk Cathedral (1525) containing stunning frescos and Sophia's tomb. A number of exhibitions occupy the lesser buildings.

The adjoining cemetery is Moscow's most prestigious and the site of the graves of the writers Anton Chekhov and Nikolai Gogol, film director Sergei Eisenstein and – curiously – Communist Party General Secretary Nikita Khrushchev, removed from power in disgrace in 1964 and hence denied a plot in the Kremlin wall (*see p41*). You can buy a guide to the cemetery at the entrance gates.

In good weather, the view of the complex from across the lake is unforgettable.

The Ostankino TV Tower

Novodevichiy Proezd 1.
Tel: 499 246 8526.
Open: Wed–Mon 10am–5pm. Admission charge. Metro: Sportivnaya.

Ostankino

Painstaking restoration is slowly returning to its former glory the 18th-century summer estate of Count Nikolai Sheremetev, one of Russia's richest and most cultured noblemen. Not all the property is open to the public, but the nearby Ostankino TV tower and the Tekhnopark fully justify a trip out from the centre of town.

Ostankino Palace

Tel: 495 683 4645. Open: May–Sept Wed–Sun 10am–6pm. Closed in damp weather. Admission charge. Metro: VDNKh, then bus or trolleybus down Ulitsa Akademika Korolyova to the lake.

Italianskiy Pavilion
(Italian Pavilion)

The theatre is flanked by two antechambers, the Italian and Egyptian Pavilions, the first of which is open to visitors. The hand-printed wallpaper, gilded woodwork and stucco ornamentation hint at the luxurious premises enjoyed by the count's privileged guests.

Teatr v Ostankino
(Ostankino Theatre)

During Ostankino's heyday, the road from Moscow was lit at night by braziers for those invited to the count's legendary soirées, the focus of which was his famous Serf Theatre.

The daughter of a serf blacksmith, Praskovya Kovalyova-Zhemchugova took to the stage at the age of 11. Breaking all the taboos of high society, Count Sheremetev fell in love with her and freed her from bondage. Catherine the Great forbade the relationship, but on her death Sheremetev prevailed on her son Paul I and the couple were married in 1801. Unfortunately, Praskovya died two years later of tuberculosis: the Sklifosovskiy Hospital for the Poor in Moscow was founded in her memory.

The theatre hall is in the main body of the building. Built entirely out of wood, the palace suffers dreadfully from damp but still manages to stage performances.

Tserkov Troitsy (Church of the Trinity)
Overlooking the estate's artificial lake, the Church of the Trinity (1692) was built by a serf architect on the site of a small wooden church. Limestone decorates the five-domed brick structure whose chief glory is the intricately carved wooden iconostasis. The palace grounds to the west consist of woods and a fair.

Beautiful 'flower clock' on one of the slopes in Victory Park

Park Pobedy (Victory Park)

A comparatively recent addition to the attractions of Moscow, this park is certainly worth visiting. It is a little way out from the centre, but it is easily reached by metro, trolleybus or car. Dominated by its obelisk and museum, Park Pobedy covers over 9ha (22 acres) and was built to commemorate the 50th anniversary of Russian victory in the Great Patriotic War of 1941–5. To reach the museum, pass through the large Victory Square, which has a row of fountains and five marble blocks, each representing a year of struggle against Nazi Germany. After a pleasant walk, visitors reach a massive obelisk 141.8m (465ft) high – representing 10cm (4 inches) for every day Russia was at war.

Right behind the obelisk is a pair of World War II cannon, standing by the entrance to the museum. Allow at least two hours in this immense building – even longer if you have a special interest in military history. Displays include Russian, German and even Japanese military equipment. The panoramic life-sized sets representing major battles and sieges are breathtaking. Visiting the Central Hall of Glory, containing the names of all Heroes of the Soviet Union, and the Memorial Hall – where books name every citizen of the USSR who fell in the war – can be a deeply emotional experience.

Right next to the museum is an open-air display of World War II tanks, cannons, trains and planes. The church of St George, Bringer of

The obelisk dominating Victory Park

Victory, is on the main Victory Square, alongside a memorial mosque and synagogue.

Victory Park should be visited twice: once during the day to visit the museum and see newlyweds come to pay homage to the victims of war, and then at night to enjoy the warm breeze of a Moscow evening and to see the fountains illuminated in red for the blood spilt in 1941–5. In summer, the park is busy until well past midnight with people roller-skating, strolling or just enjoying a drink.

If you happen to be in Moscow on 9 May, you can join tens of thousands of Russians here celebrating National Victory Day – the main public holiday, since every Russian has a relative who suffered in the war. Festivities in Victory Park include concerts, speeches by veterans and fireworks, and they last all day and late into the night.

Children may enjoy a nearby amusement park, which has numerous rides. Despite its somewhat gloomy subject, Victory Park has become a firm favourite among tourists and locals alike.

Central Museum open: Tue–Sun 10am–6pm. Closed: last Thur of month. Metro: Park Pobedy.

The Hall of Glory in the Central Museum of the Great Patriotic War

Ostankinskaya Telebashnya (Ostankino TV Tower)

At 540m (1,771ft), the world's third-tallest freestanding tower after Toronto's CN tower and Dubai's Burj Tower, the Ostankino TV mast was also the scene of the most vicious gunfire during the uprising of October 1993 (note the pockmarks in the nearby trees). Almost destroyed by fire in August 2000, it needed massive reconstruction and reopened in 2004, though not for the general public. *www.tvtower.ru. Trolleybus 13 from metro VDNKh takes you directly there.*

Park Pobedy

Borodinskaya Bitva Panorama (Borodino Battle Panorama)

As well as original and replica artefacts connected with the Napoleonic invasion, there is a huge panorama here

The Church of St George, Victory Park

depicting scenes from the Battle of Borodino in 1812. Although the heyday of panoramas is past, this one is remarkable: 115m (377ft) long and 15m (49ft) high, the painting includes about 3,000 figures. Behind the museum is a replica of the hut where Marshal Kutuzov took the momentous decision to abandon Moscow before the advancing Napoleonic army.

Desperate Russian resistance scotched Napoleon's expectations of an easy victory on the fields of Borodino in 1812, a battle celebrated in this vast panorama. The huge losses suffered on both sides made Borodino a symbol of Russia's struggle against foreign invasion. *Kutuzovskiy Prospekt 38.*
Tel: 495 148 1967.
Open: Sat–Thur 10am–5pm.
Admission charge. Metro: Park Pobedy.

Khram Svyatovo Georigya Pobedonostsa (Church of St George, Bringer of Victory)

The church was built in the 1990s to commemorate all victims of World War II in the Soviet Union. It is a small but beautiful church with the characteristic golden cupola and rich interior. The nearby memorial mosque and synagogue may also be visited.

Ploshchad Pobedy (Victory Square)

This large square dominates Park Pobedy (Victory Park). It is a favourite destination at weekends, and numerous benches next to large fountains offer a relaxing place to enjoy a snack bought at one of the nearby food stands. While walking through the square, notice the five marble blocks, each representing a year of war between 1941 and 1945. (*See also pp82–3.*)

Tsentralniy Muzey Velikoi Otechestvennoi Voenni (Central Museum of the Great Patriotic War)

This monumental museum holds a large display of World War II military artefacts and two beautiful memorial halls. At least two hours are needed to see it properly. The museum building is semicircular, supported by numerous pillars and dominated by a large dome. The impression of might is reinforced by the obelisk over 100m (328ft) tall in front of the museum. The designer Zurab Tsereteli finalised plans for the project in 1995.

Viystavka Voennoi Teckhniki (Exhibition of Military Technology)

The tanks, guns, planes and other military hardware here are all original and some are rare, such as the armoured battle trains. Visitors may see things from a soldier's point of view in the trenches by walking through a front-line military installation. There are German and Russian planes of the 1940s, but also more recent Russian fighter jets and helicopters. The display is open only in good weather.
Central Museum of the Great Patriotic War and the Exhibition of Military Technology. Tel: 495 142 4185.
Open: Tue–Sun 10am–5pm.

Tsentralniy Muzey Vooruzhennykh Sil (Central Armed Forces Museum)

Full of the hardware with which Soviet leaders threatened to 'bury the West', this excellent museum also contains memorabilia of the Red Army's most famous victories. The remains of Gary Powers's U2 spyplane, shot down in 1960, are also here. For more of the same, *see pp82–3.*
Ulitsa Sovetskoi Armii 2.
Tel: 495 681 6303. www.cmaf.ru.
Open: Wed–Sun 10am–5pm.
Admission charge. Metro: Prospekt Mira.

VVTS (All-Russian Exhibition Centre)

This grandiose park was formerly the Exhibition of Economic Achievements, a Soviet Disney World displaying a fantastically sanitised version of communist reality. Square-jawed proletarians stand over the monumental gates to 2sq km (³/₄sq mile) of kitsch pavilions once devoted to such Soviet staples as 'Metallurgy', 'Atomic Power', 'Education of the Peoples' and 'Grain'.

Today commercialism has taken over: in the Cosmos Pavilion, the Apollo-Soyuz docking craft have been shoved aside to accommodate a showroom of BMWs and Harley-Davidsons.
Tel: 495 544 3400. www.vvcentre.ru.
Open: (grounds) Mon–Fri 9am–7pm, Sat, Sun, holidays 9am–8pm; (pavilions) Mon–Fri 9am–6pm, Sat–Sun, holidays 9am–7pm. Free admission. Metro: VDNKh.

Excursions from Moscow

Once you get tired of the busy city life in Moscow and decide to get away from it all and breathe some fresh air, do not be afraid to go on some short excursions. This is a good opportunity to visit the countryside and experience a different kind of Russia. Quiet walks through the country will give you the opportunity to meet a more relaxed people than the always busy and rushing Muscovites. Trips to the country may be undertaken on your own or alternatively you can contact local excursion bureaux.

Abramtsevo

This tranquil country estate is best known as the retreat of a group of artists, 'the Wanderers' (*see pp54–5*). The railway magnate and impresario Savva Mamontov bought the house and grounds in 1870; under his patronage painters such as Ilya Repin, Mikhail Vrubel and Viktor Vasnetsov produced some of their finest work.

The Church of Our Saviour is the result of collaboration by the artists, and Mamontov is buried in the adjoining chapel.
Reach by elektrichka (90 minutes) from Yaroslavskiy Vokzal, or drive down Yaroslavskoye Shosse towards Sergiev Posad until signpost to Abramtsevo. Tel: 254 32 470. Open: Wed–Sun 10am–5pm. Closed: last Fri of month. Admission charge.

Borodino

Over 100,000 troops died in one day in 1812 on this famous battlefield, now a vast museum-reserve littered with memorials of Napoleon's plans to capture Moscow. Mass graves and trenches, testament to the 1941 bitter engagement at Borodino, are also here.

A re-enactment of the Napoleonic battle, complete with bayonet charges and cavalry, takes place every September (ask at museum).
Borodino is 124km (77 miles) from Moscow. Take elektrichka from Belorusskiy Vokzal and walk 3km (2 miles) from Borodino station to the museum. By car, take Minskoye Shosse to Mozhaisk; Borodino village is 12km (7½ miles) west. Tel: 496 385 1522. www.borodino.ru. Museum open: Tue–Sun 10am–6pm. Closed: last Fri of month. Admission charge.

Gorki Leninskie

In the heyday of Soviet power, half a million visitors a year paid homage at the estate where Lenin died, aged 53, in January 1924 after a series of strokes. Clocks in the estate are stopped at 6.50, the time of his death, and though the premises are falling into disrepair, some curios remain.

Gorki Leninskie is 35km (22 miles) south of Moscow. Take bus 439 from Domodedovskaya metro station. Alternatively, join a Patriarshy Dom Tour (tel: 495 795 0927). By car take Kashirskoye Shosse. Tel: 495 548 9309. Open: Wed–Mon 10am–5pm. Closed: last Mon of month. Admission charge.

Marfino

This peaceful village north of Moscow harbours the remains of an estate belonging to Peter the Great's tutor, Prince Golitsyn. Though spoilt by conversion into a Soviet workers' resort, the lake is a pretty summer picnic spot. *Take elektrichka from Savyolovskiy Vokzal to Katuar station (40 minutes), then catch bus 37 to estate gates. By car, drive down Dmitrovskoye Shosse until Marfino signpost.*

Melikhovo

Anton Chekhov (1860–1904) wrote his ground breaking play *The Seagull* and many short stories at his country estate here. It is a little barren in winter, but its wild gardens are enchanting in spring and summer. The buildings have been carefully preserved to evoke the writer's life.

Melikhovo is 60km (37 miles) south of Moscow. Take elektrichka from Kurskiy Vokzal to Chekhov, then bus 25. By car, drive down Varshavskoye Shosse towards Tula until the sign for Melikhovo. Chekhov estate tel: 272 23 610. Open:

Tue–Sun 10am–4pm. Closed: last Fri of month.

Peredelkino

This little village was where politically correct writers were rewarded with luxurious country retreats. Its most famous resident was Boris Pasternak (1890–1960). His house is now a museum and his nearby grave is still smothered in bouquets from a grateful nation.

Peredelkino is 25km (15½ miles) west of Moscow. Reach by elektrichka from Kievskaya Vokzal, or by road via Kutuzovskiy Prospekt and Minskoye Shosse until left turn at the 21km (13-mile) post. Tel: 495 934 5175. Pasternak's house open: Thur–Sun 10am–4pm. Admission charge.

Sergiev Posad

Formerly known as Zagorsk, this town is focused around one of Orthodox Russia's key sites, the magnificent Troitse-Sergievskaya Lavra (St Sergius Trinity Monastery).

It was founded in the 14th century by Russia's patron saint, Sergei of Radonezhskiy, who was instrumental in organising resistance to the Tartar occupation of Muscovy. Its eerie Trinity Cathedral holds a permanent service to the saint. Dress should be modest.

Sergiev Posad is 75km (46½ miles) north of Moscow. Reached by elektrichka from Yaroslavskiy Vokzal (1½ hours) or by car via Yaroslavskoye Shosse. Monastery open: daily 10am–6pm. Free admission.

ZOLOTOE KOLTSO

Zolotoe Koltso (the Golden Ring) is the name of a series of medieval towns at the very heart of Russian history. Following the decline of the great Kievan state, each became a separate principality and trading centre before the Tartar invasions and eventual absorption by Muscovy.

Each destination in the following list takes at least a day to explore, so you should plan a trip carefully. Day trips from Moscow are also possible (with the possible exception of Yaroslavl'), or you could move from one town to the next. Alternatively, take a bus tour from Moscow.

The main towns remain some of the best-preserved and most memorable destinations of any trip to Russia – the impregnable kremlins, exquisite churches and congested markets evoke the essence of the country's feudal past. Good hotel accommodation is available, often inside the monasteries. Detailed handbooks to the region are always available in Moscow.

Rostov Velikiy

'Rostov the Great' was founded on the shores of Ozero Nero (Lake Nero) as early as the 9th century and is famed for its outstanding fortress, or kremlin, built in the late 1600s. Within its walls are several gloriously decorated churches; outside, the Uspenskaya Tserkov (Church of the Assumption) steals the scene, while a number of ancient monasteries are within easy reach of the town centre.

Suzdal

Suzdal is the true gem of the Golden Ring, a sleepy rural town 220km (137 miles) from Moscow, packed

The historic town of Suzdal, near Moscow

with picturesque churches and rickety wooden cottages about the slow-moving Kamenka River. At its zenith, Suzdal boasted over 70 churches and monasteries, many donated by merchants grown rich on the city's fertile land.

Vladimir

Once Russia's capital, the ancient city of Vladimir is now a grubby textile and defence industry centre 180km (112 miles) east of Moscow. Today the city is racked by unemployment and pollution, but its glorious past as the headquarters of Russia's medieval strongman Yuri Dolgorukiy is still reflected in a number of architectural masterpieces. The 1158 Uspenskiy Sobor (Cathedral of the Assumption) on the heights above the river was the model for its namesake in the Moscow Kremlin. Vladimir also holds probably the last remaining example of old Russian military architecture – the Golden Gate built in the early 12th century.

Yaroslavl

In 2010, Yaroslavl will celebrate the 1,000th anniversary of its founding. Established as a trading post on the Volga River, Yaroslavl is the largest of the Golden Ring cities. Like its neighbours, it was ransacked by the Tartars but emerged as a flourishing princedom hosting English and Dutch traders travelling to Moscow from Arkhangel'sk on the White Sea. Fortified monasteries and the lavish

17th-century Tserkov Ioana Zlatousta (Church of St John Chrysostom) recall its former days of mercantile splendour.

If you are an ice-hockey fan, make sure you visit a home game of the local Lokomotiv Yaroslavl ice-hockey team, who have won the national ice-hockey championships three times.

Zvenigorod

The hilltop city of Zvenigorod was founded at the end of the 13th century in what is known as the 'Russian Switzerland', a lovely landscape at its best as the leaves turn with the onset of winter.

On the road heading out of town, note the remains of the kremlin, climbing from the Moskva River. A footpath leads up to the graceful Uspenskaya Tserkov (Church of the Assumption, 1396). A little further up the road lies the magnificent white-stone Savvino-Strozhevskiy monastery. It was closed down in 1919, but the gatehouse church and the monastery cathedral are being restored. Andrey Rublyov, greatest of Russia's icon masters, decorated the cathedral, and in 1918 three of his original icons were discovered in a woodshed on the hilltop. They are now on view in Moscow's Tretyakov Gallery (*see pp54–5*).

Zvenigorod is 90 minutes by elektrichka from Belorusskiy Vokzal or one hour by car along Uspenskoye Shosse. Monastery open: Tue–Sun 10am–5pm.
Admission charge.

Country life

A short ride on a suburban train leaves behind the city's emerging sophistication and takes the traveller back in time to an entirely different world – the Russian countryside.

Vast expanses of farmland, isolated cottages huddled under the severe northern sky, and headscarved women sitting beneath brightly decorated window frames watching strangers with a wary eye; this is a picture that changes little the length and breadth of Russia.

The almost idyllic scenes often conceal a life of extreme hardship. The stoicism of the Russian *muzhik* – peasant – is legendary, facing changes in politics and the weather with the same dour patience. The older among them vividly remember the terror and famines of one of Stalin's most senseless policies, collectivisation, from which country life is only now beginning to recover.

Historians reckon that 14 million were killed in the 1930s, either by

A rural homestead in the Moscow region

Autumnal tranquillity in the Russian countryside

starvation, by firing squad or in exile, as a result of the forcible destruction of private farming to create gigantic collective farms and communist 'agrotowns'. Wealthy peasants, dubbed *kulaki* or 'tight fists', were singled out for special treatment: 'We must smash the kulaks, eliminate them as a class,' Stalin ordered.

Those who resisted were sent to labour camps in Siberia or shot in their villages. Stealing one ear of corn was classified as robbing the state and punishable by up to ten years' imprisonment. One boy, Pavlik Morozov, who denounced his father for hoarding grain, was held aloft as an example to Soviet children. Streets are still named after him in Moscow.

For all its suffering, the village community is still at the heart of the Russian nation. Before the Revolution, 90 per cent of the population lived in the country. Most of today's city-dwellers are only two or three generations removed from the fields – perhaps accounting for the popular saying that Moscow is 'just one big village'.

Sankt Peterburg (St Petersburg)

St Petersburg, cultural capital of Russia, was founded in 1703, when Peter the Great snatched a soldier's bayonet and cut a cross in the soggy turf of an island in the Neva River. He probably did not say 'Here a city begins!' because at first he planned just a fort and harbour. Only later did he add a town.

Now the streets are granite, the palaces are marble, Peter's equestrian statue is bronze and the city is on the tourist map. For years the city was neglected in favour of Moscow, but, for its 300th anniversary in 2003, President Vladimir Putin relaunched his home town. That did not come cheaply. About £1 billion was spent repainting, restoring and reopening the western portal of the Mosque, rooms in the Russian Academy of Sciences, the Mikhailovskiy Garden, the Hermitage entrance from Palace Square and rooms of the Pushkinskiy Dom.

St Petersburg celebrated its 300th anniversary with laser shows, an aqua-bike show, a regatta on the Neva, gala concerts, a daytime firework display, multicoloured balloons, an international festival of military brass bands and a rock concert, as well as a 50-hour dance marathon.

President Putin gave a warm welcome to the EU leaders who gathered in St Petersburg for the EU–Russia summit in the Constantine Palace in Strelna.

The politics of a name

During World War I, the city's name was changed to the less Germanic 'Petrograd'. In 1924 the Bolsheviks

BRIDGE OPENING TIMES

When moving around the city at night, keep in mind the times when bridges over the Neva are opened to let shipping through (*see below*). If you get stuck, your only hope is to bargain with a boatman to ferry you across.

Most Aleksandra Nevskovo *2.20–5.10am*
Birzhevoi Most *2–4.55am*
Dvortsoviy Most *1.35–2.55am, 3.15–4.50am*
Grenaderskiy Most *2.45–3.45am, 4.20–4.50am*
Kantemirovskiy Most *2.45–3.45am, 4.20–4.50am*
Most Leytenanta Shmidta *1.40–4.55am*
Liteiniy Most *1.40–4.45am*
Most Petra Velikovo (Bolsheokhtinskiy) *2.45–4.55am*
Sampsonievskiy Most *2.10–2.45am, 3.20–4.25am*
Troitskiy Most *1.40–4.50am*
Tuchkov Most *2–2.55am, 3.35–4.55am*
Volodarskiy Most *2–3.45am, 4.15–5.45am*

St Petersburg town plan

Metro Stop
Cathedral
Information
Police Station
Airport
Railway Stn
Hospital
POI

500 metres
500 yards

Kitov Islands
Kizhi, Valaam

PETROGRAD SIDE
PROSPEKT DOBROLYUBOVA

Andreevskiy Sobor,
Buddiyskiy Khram, Kronstadt

Voenno-Istoricheskiy Muzey
Petropavlovskaya Krepost
ZAYACHIY OSTROV

Sampsonievskiy Sobor
Finlyandskiy
Ploshchad Lenina

Kreyser Avrora

Muzey Politicheskoi Istorii Rossii

Mechet

Smolniy Monastyr
Smolniy Institut

Muzey Muzyki v Sheremetevskom Dvortse

SVERDLOVSKAYA NAB
BOLSHEOKHTINSKIY MOST
MALOOKHTINSKIY PROSPEKT

Kikiny Palaty

SMOLNIY DISTRICT

STAVROPOLSKAYA ULITSA
SHPALERNAYA ULITSA
TVERSKAYA ULITSA
PROLETARSKOI DIKTATURY PLOSHCHAD
KAVALERGARDSKAYA UL

Bashnya
Tavricheskiy Dvorets
TAVRICHESKAYA ULITSA
SUVOROVSKIY PROSPEKT
MYTNINSKAYA ULITSA
PROSPEKT BAKUNINA

Aleksandro-Nevskiy Lavra
Cemeteries
MOST ALEKSANDRA NEVSKOVO

Neva

ARSENALNAYA NABEREZHNAYA
SMOLNAYA NABEREZHNAYA

UTENIY MOST
LITEYNIY MOST

SHPALERNAYA ULITSA
ULITSA CHAYKOVSKOVO
ZAKHARYEVSKAYA ULITSA
FURSHTADSKAYA ULITSA
Ploshchad Chernyshevskovo
PREOBRAZHENSKAYA
KIROCHNAYA ULITSA

ROBESPERA NABEREZHNAYA
POTEMKINSKAYA ULITSA
SUVOROVSKIY PROSPEKT

ULITSA VOSSTANIYA
Ploshchad Vosstaniya
Moskovskiy
Oktyabrskiy

PROSPEKT BAKUNINA
MIRGORODSKAYA ULITSA
KREMENCHUGSKAYA UL
NEVSKIY PROSPEKT
KHERSONSKAYA UL

KUTUZOVA NABEREZHNAYA
Letniy Sad
Muzey Blokada Leningrada
SOLYANOI PER
MOKHOVAYA ULITSA
LITEYNIY PROSPEKT

MAYAKOVSKOVO
ULITSA MAYAKOVSKOVO
Literaturno-Memorialny Muzey Anny Akhmatovoi
Muzey Muzyki v Sheremetevskom Dvortse

Sobor Vladimiskoi Bogomateri
Vladimirskaya
Literaturno-Memorialny Muzey F M Dostoevskovo
ULITSA LOMONOSOVA

Pavlovsk, Tsarskoe Selo

PETROVSKAYA NABEREZHNAYA
TROITSKIY MOST

REKI MOYKI NAB
Mikhailovskiy Sad
Khram Spasa na Krovi
Russkiy Muzey

Fontanka
REKI FONTANKI NAB

Rossiyskiy Etnograficheskiy Muzey
PLOSHCHAD ISKUSSTV
SADOVAYA UL
ITALYANSKAYA

Rimsko-Katolicheskaya Tserkov Svyatoi Ekateriny
Gostiny Dvor
NEVSKIY PROSPEKT
Muzey Teatralnovo Muzykalnovo Iskusstva
VLADIMIRSKIY PR
Dostoevskaya
PEREULOK DZHAMBULA
PEREULOK TYUSHINA
Vitebsky
ZAGORODNIY PROSPEKT

STRELKA
Ermitazh
DVORTSOVAYA NAB
DVORTSOVY MOST
Voenno Morskoi Muzey
Zoologicheskiy Muzey
BIRZHEVOI MOST
Muzey Antropologii i Etnografii

Universitet Sankt-Peterburg (Zdánie Dvenadtsati Kollegy)
UNIVERSITETSKAYA NAB

VASILEVSKIY OSTROV
Bolshaya Neva
Menshikovskiy Dvorets

Muzey-Kvartira A S Pushkina
Glavniy Shtab
PLOSHCHAD DEKABRISTOV
Uyteranskaya Tserkov Svyatovo Petra
Isaakievskiy Sobor
ISAAKIEVSKAYA PLOSHCHAD
ADMIRALTEYSKAYA NAB
Admiralteystvo

Stroganovskiy Dvorets
KAZANSKAYA ULITSA
Sobor Kazanskoi Bogomateri
Kazanskaya

GOROKHOVAYA ULITSA
GOROKHOVAYA ULITSA
SADOVAYA ULITSA
Sennaya Ploshchad
Sadovaya
Spasskaya

ULITSA LOMONOSOVA
REKI FONTANKI NAB
Muzey Zheleznodorozhnovo Transporta
Pushkinskaya
MOSKOVSKIY
MOSKOVSKIY PROSPEKT
Pulkovo

Malaya Neva
TUCHKOV MOST
Sportivnaya

BOLSHAYA NEVA
NABEREZHNAYA MAKAROVA

MOST LEYTENANTA SHMIDTA
Petehof

Muzey V V Nabokova
Mariinskiy Teatr
Sinagoga
TEATRALNAYA PLOSHCHAD
GLINKI ULITSA
LERMONTOVSKIY PROSP
Nikolskiy Morskoi Sobor
MOYKI
ANGLIYSKAYA NAB
REKI MOYKI NAB
VOZNESENSKIY PR
KRYUKOVA KANALA NAB
GRIBOEDOVA KANALA NAB
UL TRUDA
BOLSHAYA MORSKAYA UL
GOROKHOVAYA ULITSA

N

renamed it 'Leningrad'. The name 'St Petersburg' was readopted by referendum in 1991 when the flush of anti-Soviet enthusiasm was at its most passionate, but many of its five million inhabitants continue to call the city Leningrad.

NORTH OF NEVSKIY PROSPEKT
Armyanskaya Tserkov (Armenian Church)

A classical building built in 1771–80 by Yuri Velten.
Nevskiy Prospekt 40–42.
Metro: Nevskiy Prospekt.

Dvortsovaya Ploshchad (Palace Square)

The footsteps of Imperial Guards and revolutionary detachments no longer echo across the square, yet this stage on which the drama of Russian history has played still readily conjures up its restless past.

Enclosed by the Winter Palace (Zimniy Dvorets) and the General Staff building, Palace Square was the tsars' favourite military parade ground. It was also the epicentre of the Revolutions of 1917 that heralded the end of Romanov rule.

The 1905 Revolution began on 'Bloody Sunday', when a crowd marched on the square petitioning Nicholas II to improve living and working conditions. Hundreds were killed when guards opened fire on the peaceful demonstrators, fatally wounding the weak tsar's image as the people's 'Beloved Father'.

On 25 October 1917, night of the Bolshevik Revolution, the square was the scene of the capture of the Winter Palace by Red Guards under Trotsky's command (*see pp14–15*). Their aim was to arrest the Provisional Government, unsuccessfully defended by 300 Cossacks.

The American journalist John Reed asked an opposition politician whether the insurrection would succeed: 'The Devil knows!' he replied. 'Well, perhaps the Bolsheviks can seize power, but they won't be able to hold it more than three days ... Perhaps it's a good thing to let them try – that will finish them ...'

Today the square is a favourite venue for political meetings and popular entertainment.

Palace Square and Alexander Column

Aleksandrovskaya Kolonna (Alexander Column)

The Alexander Column in the centre of the square is dedicated to Tsar Alexander I for his role in the triumph over Napoleon. The inscription on this monument to the defeat of Napoleon reads: 'To Alexander the First from a Grateful Russia'.

The column was designed by Auguste de Montferrand in 1829. It took over a year to haul the 600-tonne (590-ton) monolith, at 47.5m (156ft) high the largest of its kind in the world, from a Finnish quarry to St Petersburg. Over 2,000 soldiers and war veterans, cheered on by a huge crowd and watched by Nicholas I, pulled it on to the pedestal where it remains. Thanks to the original system of scaffolding and winches, developed by the French engineer Agustin de Betancourt, it took only two hours to lift the column on to the pedestal. It is not fastened to its foundation; due to accurate calculations, it is held in its place by its own weight.

Glavniy Shtab (General Staff Building)

To the south, Palace Square is flanked by a grand structure, built to house the General Staff and the ministries of foreign affairs and finance. These enormous edifices are united by a monumental arch spanning Bolshaya Morskaya Street.

It was not easy to arrange the 600m (1,969ft) façade – then the longest in Europe – in such a simple and expressive way. Carlo Rossi (1775–1849) skilfully solved the task, accentuating the central part by a majestic arch, conceived as a monument to the Patriotic War of 1812. The arch is decorated with representations of armour and flying glories and topped with Victory driving a six-horse chariot. Today it houses part of the Hermitage Museum.

Zimniy Dvorets (Winter Palace)

The tsars' stunning winter residence, the fourth Winter Palace, was completed by Bartolomeo Rastrelli in 1762. After 1881 Alexander III moved to Gatchina and the Winter Palace was used only on especially solemn occasions. For a few months in 1917 the palace was the home of the Provisional Government. It is considered the masterpiece of Russian Baroque architecture, created, in Rastrelli's own words, 'exclusively to glorify Russia'.

Most of the interior, apart from the elegant Jordan Staircase, has been remodelled since Rastrelli's time according to the whim of passing tsars. The palace was almost entirely burnt to the ground in the fire of December 1837 but was completely rebuilt by Easter 1839.

Its staggeringly opulent state rooms and halls now function as what is probably the world's most luxurious art gallery (*pp100–103*).
Metro: Nevskiy Prospekt, then trolleybus 1, 5, 7, 10 or 22.

Waterways

One of the world's most beautiful maritime cities, St Petersburg is defined by the River Neva, which gave the city its first harbour. It was built to open Russia to sea trade with northwest Europe. The first ship sailed up the Neva in November 1703. Tsar Peter was so overjoyed that he rowed out to pilot it personally, before buying the whole cargo of wine and salt. He gave the captain 500 gold roubles and, when the Dutchman explained that he was bound for the Swedish port of Narva, Peter offered

A boat approaches the Anichkov Bridge

A boat passes the Winter Palace on the River Neva

him another 300 roubles to return promptly.

The Neva's south bank is drained by a series of concentric canals and rivers. At times the elements have proved to be too much for them, though. Catherine the Great awoke on the morning of the great flood of 1777 to be told that her wing of the Winter Palace was about to be submerged.

The waterways offer enchanting views of St Petersburg – often called 'the Venice of the North' because it is built on 44 islands, linked by over 600 bridges. During the shipping season, from 19 April until 30 September, various boat trips allow you to see palaces, churches, monuments, gardens and bridges. The trips vary from 40 minutes to 1 hour and cost from about 450 roubles.

Walk: Nevskiy Prospekt

Nevskiy Prospekt was laid out in the early days of the city and was first known as the Great Perspective Road, running 4.5km (3 miles) from the Admiralty to the Alexander Nevskiy Monastery. This main artery reveals a wealth of attractive buildings.

Allow 1 hour.

1 Admiralteystvo (The Admiralty)

A fortified shipyard was built on this site in 1704–11 by architect Andreyan Zakharov. It has been occupied by the Naval Engineering School since 1925.

2 Literaturnoe Kafe (Literary Café)

Once the 'Wolf and Béranger', this café was known for its fashionable clientele. Pushkin left from here for his fatal duel in 1837.

3 Stroganovskiy Dvorets (Stroganov Palace)

(*See p120.*)

4 Lyuteranskaya Tserkov Petra (Lutheran Church of St Peter)

(*See p108.*)

5 Sobor Kazanskoi Bogomateri (Cathedral of Our Lady of Kazan)

This is an outstanding example of early 19th-century Russian architecture. Tsar Paul I modelled it on St Peter's in Rome (*see p120*).

6 Dom Knigi (The House of Books)

Built for the Singer Sewing Machine Company in 1902–4 by Pavel Syuzor in art nouveau style, this is the biggest bookshop in the city today.

Turn left off Nevskiy Prospekt and head up Griboyedova Kanala Naberezhnaya.

7 Khram Spasa na Krovi (Church on the Spilt Blood)

This church was built in 1887–1907. Over 20 types of minerals are lavished on the interior (*see p108*).

Return along the Naberezhnaya and turn left to continue along Nevskiy Prospekt.

8 Maliy Zal Filarmonii (Small Hall of the State Academic Philharmonic)

This was the main concert hall of the city from 1826 to 1846.

9 Tserkov Svyatoi Ekateriny (Roman Catholic Church of St Catherine)

(*See p109.*)

10 Gostiny Dvor

Strictly neoclassical in outline, this bazaar was completed in 1785 and now has more than 300 shops.

11 Rossiyskaya Natsionalnaya Biblioteka (Russian National Library)

The library was opened in 1814 and is the fifth-largest library in the world.
Turn right off Nevskiy Prospekt and cross Ploshchad Ostrovskovo.

12 Aleksandrinskiy Teatr (Aleksandrinskiy Theatre)

The theatre was built in 1828–32 by Carlo Rossi.
Retrace your steps and turn right on Nevskiy Prospekt.

13 Anichkovskiy Dvorets (Anichkov Palace)

Built in 1816–18, this was a gift from Tsarina Elizabeth to her lover Aleksey Razumovskiy. It now houses the Palace of Youth Creativity.

14 Anichkovskiy Most (Anichkov Bridge)

It is famous for its four bronze statues of men taming horses by Peter Klodt.

15 Beloselskikh-Belozerskikh Dvorets (Beloselskiy-Belozerskiy Palace)

Designed by Stakenschneider in 1847–8, this is now a cultural centre.

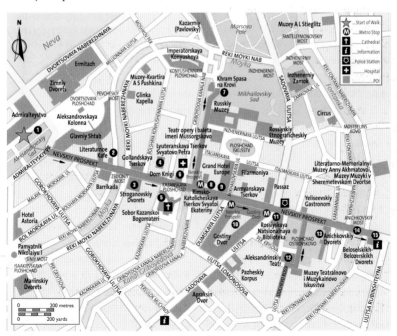

St Petersburg

Ermitazh
(State Hermitage Museum)

This is one of the world's truly great art museums. Among the Hermitage's treasures are artworks by Leonardo da Vinci, Raphael, Titian, Rembrandt and Rubens, a celebrated collection of Impressionist and post-Impressionist paintings, not to mention work by Matisse and Picasso. World renowned are the collections of Scythian gold and the antiquities from the shores of the Black Sea.

The story of the Hermitage begins with Peter the Great, who brought back paintings from foreign tours and showed them in the Russian Museum (*see pp110–11*). But it was during the reign of Catherine the Great that the collection really took shape. In 1764 she received 225 works from the Berlin merchant Gotzkowsky, who had made the collection for the Prussian king Frederick II, who, owing to reverses in the Seven Years War, had to put the collection up for sale. The collections of Baron de Thiers and the British prime minister Sir Robert Walpole, which she also acquired, included large numbers of European masters.

Catherine allowed only selected guests to view the works, and it was not until the October Revolution of 1917 that the doors of the Hermitage opened to the people. After the Revolution, many private collections were added to the Imperial one. As a specified German target, the museum's treasures were evacuated to the Urals

during World War II. Today the Hermitage Museum comprises six buildings: the Small Hermitage, the Old (Large) Hermitage, the New Hermitage, the Hermitage Theatre, part of the General Staff Building and the Winter Palace.

Dvortsovaya Naberezhnaya 34. Tel: 710 9079. www.hermitagemuseum.org. Open: Tue–Sat 10.30am–6pm, Sun 10.30am–5pm. Admission charge. Free first Thur of month. Tours available in English. Metro: Nevskiy Prospekt, then trolleybus 1, 5, 7, 10 or 22.

Viewing the collection

To spend just one minute looking at each of the exhibits would take over 12 years, so a visit should be planned carefully to avoid severe picture fatigue. The panel on the left outlines the main order of the exhibition, which occupies the former Winter Palace (entered through the chief Neva embankment entrance) and the Small and Large Hermitages.

The Hermitage hosts temporary exhibitions, advertised in the foyer.

The Golden Rooms

It has taken over two centuries to assemble the unique collection of gold, silver and gems fashioned into fascinating pieces of jewellery by Russian, European and Oriental artists and craftsmen. The gold of the Nomads is represented by unique finds from the north coast of the Black Sea, the northern Caucases and western Siberia. Greek gold from the shores of the Black Sea is also featured. The jewellery art of the East and of South America is unknown to most people and very rare.

The State Rooms

The State Rooms of the tsars' Winter Palace are a breathtaking display of Imperial elegance. The Main Staircase, left from the ticket offices, leads majestically to the Antechamber, Nicholas Hall and Concert Hall before you arrive at the Malachite Room (room 189) where the Provisional Government convened before they

Much of the Hermitage Museum is housed in the Winter Palace

were ousted by the Bolsheviks in the 1917 Revolution.

Alternatively, turn right at the top of the staircase and head through the Field Marshals' Hall to Peter's Throne Room and the Armorial Hall. A door to the left leads to the 1812 Corridor, lined with paintings of the field commanders who defeated Napoleon, and through to the magnificent St George's Hall (room 198), adorned with a mosaic map of the USSR set with semi-precious stones.

Prehistory and antiquity
Occupying much of the ground floor, the Hermitage's collection includes a number of Egyptian mummies and sarcophagi and a display of classical artefacts – delicate cameos, terracotta figurines, mosaics, fine statuary, etc.

Russian art and culture
The collection consists of over 300,000 items and reflects a 1,000-year Russian history. This section is devoted mostly to icons, ceramics and furniture, old books and archaeological finds that represent the inner world and way of life of ancient Russia. (Russian painting is largely confined to the Russian Museum – *see pp110–11.*)

The New Hermitage building

Highlights of the Picture Gallery

Among the countless paintings, look out for the following delights listed below. Displays change very infrequently.

English *The Infant Heracles Killing Snakes* by Joshua Reynolds, room 300.
Portrait of a Lady in Blue by Thomas Gainsborough, room 298.

Dutch and Flemish *Perseus and Andromeda, Feast at the House of Simon the Pharisee* and *Bacchus* by Peter Paul Rubens, room 247.
Portrait of Charles I and *Virgin with Partridges* by Anthony Van Dyck, room 246.
Danae, Abraham Sacrificing Isaac and *The Return of the Prodigal Son* by Rembrandt, room 254.

French *Tancred and Erminia* and *Landscape with Polyphemus* by Nicolas Poussin, room 279.
The Stolen Kiss by Jean-Honoré Fragonard, room 288.

Italian *Madonna and Child with Sts Dominic and Thomas Aquinas* by Fra Angelico, room 209.
Madonna with a Flower and *Madonna and Child* by Leonardo da Vinci, room 214.
Danae and *The Repentant Mary Magdalene* by Titian, room 221.
Lamentation by Paolo Veronese, room 222.

Madonna Conestabile by Raphael, room 229.

Spanish *The Apostles Peter and Paul* by El Greco, room 240.
The Luncheon by Diego Velázquez, room 239.
Portrait of Antonia Zarate by Francisco de Goya, room 239.

Modern European art

Do not miss the wonderful collection of Impressionist and post-Impressionist works, including paintings by van Gogh, Monet and Renoir, and the famous canvases by Picasso and Matisse. The latter were acquired from the collections of two Russian philanthropists, Ivan Morozov and Sergey Shchukin, who kept the artists solvent early in their careers.

Woman Holding a Fruit by Paul Gauguin, room 316.
The Lilac Bush and *Cottages* by Vincent van Gogh, room 317.
Still Life with Curtain and *The Smoker* by Paul Cézanne, room 318.
A Lady in a Garden and *Waterloo Bridge: Effect of Fog* by Claude Monet, room 319.
Portrait of the Actress Jeanne Samary by Auguste Renoir, room 320.
Woman Combing Her Hair by Edgar Degas, room 326.
The Dance and *The Red Room* by Henri Matisse, rooms 344–5.
The Absinthe Drinker and *Sisters* by Pablo Picasso, room 348.

Walk: The Winter Palace to the Summer Garden

This short stroll encompasses the sites of two regicides, the home of Russia's greatest poet, two royal palaces and the Summer Garden.

Allow 2 hours.

Start on the eastern side of Dvortsovaya Ploshchad (Palace Square, see pp94–5).

1 Moyka River

Crossing Pevcheskiy Most (Singers' Bridge) to the right bank of the Moyka, you are faced with the Glinka Kapella, St Petersburg's oldest concert hall and once headquarters of the Imperial Court Choir. A little further on, at Reki Moyki Naberezhnaya 12, Russia's national poet Alexander Pushkin lived in the first-floor apartments (*see pp108–9*).
Continue across the square to the bridge over the Griboyedova Canal.

2 Khram Spasa na Krovi (Church on the Spilt Blood)

(*See p108.*)
Head north, once more crossing the Moyka.

3 Marsovo Pole (The Field of Mars)

The open expanse north of the Moyka became an Imperial parade ground. The eternal flame in the centre honours the 180 dead of the 1917 February Revolution buried here, and the fallen of the October Revolution and civil war.

The Mramorniy Dvorets (Marble Palace) of 1785 at the far end of the square was built for Catherine the Great's lover Count Grigori Orlov, who lost it twice gambling at cards. *Enter the Summer Garden through the wrought-iron grille from the embankment.*

4 Letniy Sad and Letniy Dvorets (Summer Garden and Palace)

The recently refurbished Summer Garden was laid out informally after a flood in 1777 washed away Peter the Great's more ambitious pastiche of the gardens of Versailles. Peter's Summer Palace (1710) is characteristically modest. His wife lived on the first floor while Peter busied himself at his lathe in the turnery or at raucous banquets below. The park is more tranquil than in Peter's day, when he would order the nobility to join in 'drinking assemblies'.
Letniy Sad open: daily summer 10am–10pm; winter 10am–dusk. Admission charge in summer.

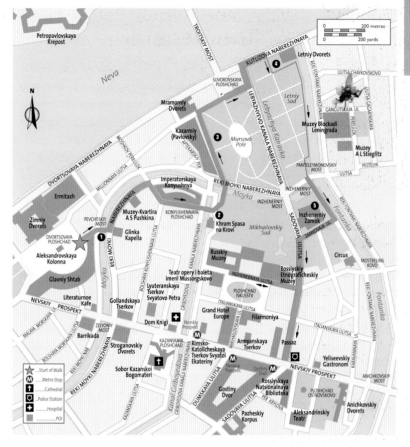

Letniy Dvorets *tel: 314 0456. Open: May–Oct Mon 10am–4pm, Wed–Sun 10am–5pm. Closed: last Mon of month. Admission charge. Leaving the Summer Garden, take the Fontanka left bank to the Engineers' Castle.*

5 Inzhenerniy Zamok (Engineers' Castle)

The Engineers' Castle (1801) was once surrounded by a moat to protect Paul I,

who was terrified of assassination. He died mere days after he had moved in, throttled in his nightshirt by courtiers and army officers exasperated by their tsar's accelerating insanity. The building takes its name from the Engineering Academy to which it was transferred. Today this building belongs to the Russian Museum.

A short walk south brings you to Nevskiy Prospekt or Ploshchad Iskusstv and the Russian Museum (see pp110–11).

The Siege

For everyone living in St Petersburg, the Siege (*Blokada*) of Leningrad is an important part of their heritage; for older generations it brings terrible memories. The most tragic period in the city's history was full of suffering and heroism.

Hitler hoped to capture the city in September 1941. His high command even printed invitations to a banquet at Leningrad's Astoria Hotel. It never took place.

On 22 June 1941 the Soviet Union was attacked by Nazi Germany. Less than two and a half months later, German troops were approaching Leningrad and outflanked the Red Army. By 8 September 1941 the Germans encircled Leningrad and the Siege began. It lasted for 872 days.

The lives of Leningrad's citizens became a permanent struggle against fire, bombs, cold and hunger while working to defend the city, assist the injured and take care of children and elderly people. Food and fuel stocks were very limited. All public transport stopped. But the 2,887,000 civilians (including about 400,000 children) plus troops did not even consider surrender.

The unusually cold winter of 1941–2 was the biggest test, with temperatures below –30°C (–22°F). In January 1942 there were no electricity or water supplies and the daily food ration sank to 125g (about 4½oz) of bread per day. In January and February 1942, 200,000 people died in Leningrad of cold and starvation. However, despite the appalling conditions suffered by the inhabitants, the city did not surrender.

Several hundred thousand people were evacuated across Lake Ladoga via the famous 'Road of Life' – the only route out of the city. In summer, people were ferried across; in winter, lorries drove across the frozen lake under constant enemy bombardment.

In January 1943 the Siege was broken, and a year later, on 27 January 1944, it was fully lifted. At least 641,000 people (perhaps 800,000) had died. Most were buried in mass graves in cemeteries.

The Siege of Leningrad was dramatised for the world. Dmitri Shostakovich wrote his Seventh Symphony, the Leningrad Symphony, during the siege. Leningrad came to symbolise the Soviet–Nazi conflict, especially for the Americans. On 9 September 1941, after the start of relentless shelling and air raids, a BBC broadcast said: 'Listen, Leningrad! This is London calling!

London is with you. Every shot in Leningrad echoes in London.'

There is a Monument to the Heroic Defenders of Leningrad and a Memorial Museum of Leningrad Defence and the Siege, where you can see original documents and items of that time.

Detail from the Monument to the Heroic Defenders of Leningrad

Khram Spasa na Krovi (Church on the Spilt Blood)

Built on the site where Tsar Alexander II was assassinated by members of *Narodnaya Volya* (People's Will) in 1881 (hence 'on the Spilt Blood'), the design of this church is not neoclassical, as elsewhere in St Petersburg, but old Russian. After admiring the stunning mosaics and coats of arms on the exterior, be prepared to be bowled over by the interior décor, the work of Viktor Vasnetsov, Mikhail Nesterov and others.
Griboyedova Naberezhnaya 2a.
Metro: Nevskiy Prospekt.

Literaturno-Memorialnyi Muzey Anny Akhmatovoi v Fontannom Dome (Anna Akhmatova Museum at Fontanny Dom)

Dedicated to the life and work of the famous poet (*see p59*), this is the apartment where she lived from 1924 to 1952.
Reki Fontanki Naberezhnaya 34 (a wing of the Sheremetev Palace).
Tel: 579 7239. www.akhmatova.spb.ru.
Open: Tue–Sun 10.30am–6.30pm.
Closed: last Wed of month.
Metro: Mayakovskaya/Gostiny Dvor.

Lyuteranskaya Tserkov Svyatovo Petra (Lutheran Church of St Peter)

Dating from 1832–8, this is by the architect Alexander Briullov in a classical style.
Nevskiy Prospekt 22–24.
Metro: Nevskiy Prospekt.

Muzey Blockadi Leningrada (Blockade Museum)

Exhibits at this fascinating museum tell the story of the Nazi blockade of St Petersburg during World War II.
Solyanoi Pereulok 9. Tel: 275 7208.
Open: Thur–Tue 10am–5pm. Admission charge. Metro: Chernyshevskaya.

Muzey-Kvartira A S Pushkina (Alexander Pushkin Apartment Museum)

The last residence of the poetic genius, this is where he died on 29 January 1837, after his duel with Baron d'Anthès (an ardent admirer of his wife). Original books and artefacts,

The Church on the Spilt Blood

personal belongings and the original furnishings are on show.

Reki Moyki Naberezhnaya 12.
Tel: 311 3531. www.museumpushkin.ru.
Open: Wed–Mon 10.30am–5pm. Closed:
last Fri of month. Admission charge.
Metro: Nevskiy Prospekt.

Muzey Muzyki v Sheremetevskom Dvortse (Museum of Music in Sheremetev Palace) (Fontanny Dom)

This 18th-century building by the architect Savva Chevakinskiy belonged to Count Sheremetev. In the gala halls are items from the family's collections. Among them are objects of decorative and applied art of the 17th to 20th centuries. The St Petersburg collection of musical instruments (3,000 items) includes ones made by celebrated craftsmen or played by famous musicians, and historical rarities. Symphonic, choral and chamber music concerts are held in the White Hall.

Reki Fontanki Naberezhnaya 34
(next to Akhmatova Museum).
Tel: 272 3898. www.theatremuseum.ru.
Open: Wed–Sun noon–6pm. Closed: last
Wed of month. Admission charge. Metro:
Mayakovskaya/Gostiny Dvor.

Rimsko-Katolicheskaya Tserkov Svyatoi Ekateriny (Roman Catholic Church of St Catherine)

Built in 1763–83 by Vallin de la Mothe, in a mixture of Baroque and neoclassical styles.

Nevskiy Prospekt 32–34.
Metro: Nevskiy Prospekt.

Rossiyskiy Etnograficheskiy Muzey (Russian Museum of Ethnography)

The exhibits illustrate the everyday life and culture of the peoples of Russia from the 18th to the 20th centuries. There are over half a million exhibits from across the Russian Federation and the former USSR.

Inzhenernaya Ulitsa 4/1.
Tel: 570 5421. www.ethnomuseum.ru.
Open: Tue–Sun 10.30am–6pm.
Closed: last Fri of month.
Admission charge.
Metro: Nevskiy Prospekt.

Russkiy Muzey (Russian Museum)

(See pp110–11.)

SOUTH OF NEVSKIY PROSPEKT
Aleksandro-Nevskiy Lavra (Alexander Nevskiy Monastery)

This monastery was founded by Peter the Great, supposedly on the site of Prince Alexander Nevskiy's 1240 victory over the Swedes. Today, the peeling paintwork and crows fluttering above the graveyards combine to leave a haunting impression.

Blagoveshchenskaya Tserkov (Church of the Annunciation)

Designed by Peter's chief builder Domenico Trezzini, this church once

(Cont. on p114)

Russkiy Muzey (Russian Museum)

St Petersburg's superb collection of Russian art is comparable only with the Tretyakov Gallery in Moscow in quality and scale (*see pp54–5*). The Russian Museum's rooms provide a journey through the development of painting in Russia, from the earliest iconography to the avant-garde explosion and subsequent Stalinist orthodoxy of the 20th century.

Iconography

Starting with Russia's earliest art form, icon painting, rooms 1–3 on the first floor have fine examples. One of the oldest is the 12th-century Archangel Gabriel, known as *The Angel with the Golden Hair* – the angel's stylised features reflect Byzantine influences. Other highlights include the mid-14th-century icon of the murdered sons of Prince Vladimir, Sts Boris and Gleb, a stunning 15th-century

Michael's Palace houses the Russian Museum

rendition of St George fighting the Dragon, with scenes from his life, and works by the master of the genre, Andrey Rublyov.

Peter the Great and beyond

Russian art reached a watershed during the reign of Peter the Great. Thrilled by what he had seen in Western Europe, he sent promising artists abroad on scholarships to perfect their skills. Ivan Nikitin's *Portrait of the Hetman* (c1720) in room 5 and *Self-portrait with the Artist's Wife* (1729) by Andrey Matveev in room 6 illustrate the resulting break with medieval styles.

Academy of Arts

Founded in 1757, the Academy of Arts promoted classicism, emphasising subjects from history, the Bible and classical mythology. Room 9 shows an early history painting, *Vladimir and Rogneda* (1770) by Anton Losenko, depicting the horror of a Polovtsian princess after the murder of her father and brothers by her determined suitor, Prince Vladimir.

Leaps of progress in portraiture can be seen in room 10 with the work of Dmitri Levitsky, especially his canvases of Count Vorontsov (1780s) and academy director Alexander Kokorinov (1769).

Of the early 19th-century classical paintings, outstanding are Kark Bryullov's monumental *Last Day of Pompeii* (1833) and Ivan Aivazovsky's *The Ninth Wave* in room 14. Room 15 includes *The Appearance of Christ before the People* (1857), the greatest work of the academy's other hero, Alexander Ivanov.

Peredvizhniki (the Wanderers)

The group of realist artists dubbed *Peredvizhniki* was led by Ivan Kramskoi (1837–87), whose piercing portraits fill room 25. The artists set up the Association of Travelling Art Exhibitions, and came to be known as the Wanderers or Itinerants. Nikolai Ge scandalised society with the realism of his *Last Supper* (1863) in room 26. Ilya Repin is one of Russia's best-loved painters and many of his works are hung in rooms 33–5: two of the most famous are *Barge-haulers on the Volga* (1873) and the hilarious *Zaporozhe Cossacks* (1891).

Turning of the century

Russian art experienced an explosion of styles at the turn of the last century. Isaak Levitan's wistful landscapes in room 44 demonstrate his mastery of Impressionism. Philip Maliavin's *Two Girls* in room 47 is considered to be one of his best works.

In the adjoining Benois wing, look out for other major 19th- and 20th-century artists including Mikhail Vrubel in room 66, Leon Bakst (room 68), Pavel Kuznetsov (room 74) and Vasily Kandinsky (room 79). *Mikhailovskiy Dvorets, Inzhenernaya Ulitsa 4. Tel: 595 4248/314 3448. www.rusmuseum.ru/eng. Open: Wed–Sun 10am–5pm, Mon 10am–4pm. Admission charge. Metro: Nevskiy Prospekt. Entrance to the Benois Wing is from the Griboyedov Canal embankment.*

Michael's (or Engineers') Castle

Walk: The Smolniy district

Intimately connected with the events of 1917, this peaceful residential district conceals its violent history behind the tranquil Tauride Gardens and the stunning cathedral of the Smolniy Convent.

Allow 2 hours.

Start at Chernyshevskaya metro and turn right out of the metro and right again down Furshtadskaya Ulitsa.

1 Tavricheskiy Sad (Tauride Gardens)

Statues of Tchaikovsky and the poet Sergei Esenin preside over squealing children, strolling pensioners and inebriated fishermen here, one of St Petersburg's most attractive parks.

2 Tavricheskiy Dvorets (Tauride Palace)

In the far left corner of the park stands the Tauride Palace, site of the first 'Duma' or parliament in 1906 and home to the short-lived Constituent Assembly, disbanded in 1918 by the Red Guards.

Built in 1789, the palace was a gift from Catherine the Great to her lover Prince Grigory Potemkin. In one of his frequent fits of hatred for his mother, her son Paul donated the palace to the Horse Guards for stables. (Closed to the public.)

Leave the park via Tavricheskaya Ulitsa towards Shpalernaya Ulitsa.

3 Bashnya ('The Tower')

Building No 35 on the corner of Tverskaya Ulitsa is famed for its top-floor apartment, dubbed 'The Tower'. It was the meeting place of one of Russia's greatest avant-garde circles, including the poets Anna Akhmatova, Alexander Blok, Osip Mandelstam and Nikolai Gumilyov. Most of them were exiled, executed or silenced by the Bolsheviks.

Head right down Shpalernaya Ulitsa.

4 Kikiny Palaty (Kikin's Chambers)

The view of the Smolniy Cathedral is breathtaking as you approach the convent along Shpalernaya Ulitsa, but it is worth looking at the beautifully preserved building on the left near the junction with Stavropolskaya Ulitsa. It briefly belonged to one of Peter the Great's senior bureaucrats, Alexander Kikin, before he suffered public torture and execution on Moscow's Red Square for befriending Peter's estranged son.

5 Smolniy Monastyr (Smolniy Convent)

One of St Petersburg's highlights, the icy grandeur of the Smolniy Convent is the work of the great architect Bartolomeo Rastrelli. The design, commissioned by Tsarina Elizabeth in 1748, originally included a vertiginous 140m (459ft) bell tower, now reduced to 63m (207ft). The convent's brief religious life – in 1797 it became a home for widows of the nobility – may explain the unimaginative cathedral interior. You can climb up the bell tower to enjoy the view over the Neva.

(The name 'Smolniy' (*smola* – tar) is derived from the shipbuilders' tar yards

on the site in Peter's time.)
Open: Thur–Tue 10am–5.30pm.
Admission charge.

6 Smolniy Institut (Smolniy Institute)

Adjoining the convent, the former Smolniy Institute was Russia's first school for girls, but is better known as the nerve centre from which Trotsky and Lenin plotted the Bolshevik Revolution. It also witnessed the murder of Party boss Sergei Kirov in 1934, marking the inception of Stalin's savage purges. (Closed to the public.)
Return along Suvorovskiy Prospekt by trolleybus 5, 7, 11 or 16 to Ploshchad Vosstaniya metro.

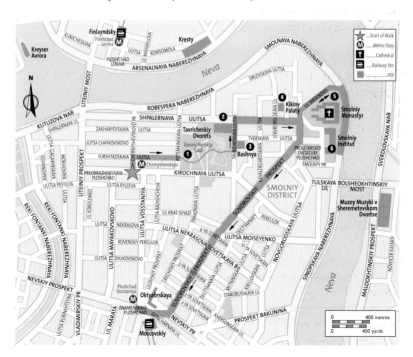

served as the Romanovs' necropolis and still contains the tombs of Russia's greatest military mind, General Alexander Suvorov (1730–1800), and Catherine the Great's leading statesman, Prince Alexander Golitsyn. The adjoining monastery buildings, fine examples of Petrine architecture, are closed to the public.

Cemeteries

A gateway in the right-hand wall of the drive leads to the Tikhvinskoe Kladbishche (Tikhvin Cemetery), containing the graves of some of Russia's greatest artists, including the writer Fyodor Dostoevsky and the composers Modest Mussorgsky and Nikolay Rimsky-Korsakov. In the far right corner, a harrowing bust captures the exhausted soul of Pyotr Ilych Tchaikovsky, who committed suicide in 1893.

Opposite, the Lazarus Cemetery is the resting place of the aristocracy but also contains the graves of the polymath Mikhail Lomonosov, Pushkin's wife Natalya Goncharova and many of the city's architects.

Troitskiy Sobor (Cathedral of the Trinity)

Catherine the Great's taste for classicism created a headache for the architect Ivan Starov. Yet he succeeded – the vast interior (1790) retains an Orthodox intimacy. The remains of Alexander Nevskiy, canonised by the Church, lie to the right of the iconostasis. (Women should cover their heads.)

The dome of St Isaac's Cathedral dominates the skyline

Ploshchad Aleksandra Nevskovo.
Tel: 274 1702. Monastery open: daily
dawn–dusk. Free admission.
Tikhvin Cemetery and Lazarus Cemetery
open: Fri–Wed 10am–5pm.
Admission charge. Metro: Ploshchad
Aleksandra Nevskovo.

Isaakievskaya Ploshchad (St Isaac's Square)

Begun in the 1730s, this was the last of
the central squares to take shape in
St Petersburg.

Hotel Astoria

One of St Petersburg's leading hotels
was designed by F Lidval in 1910–12
in art nouveau style. Hitler had
planned a banquet in the hotel, but his
dreams of conquest did not come true.
From 1987 to 1991 the Astoria
underwent major refurbishment
while staying faithful to the original
style of the building.

Isaakievskiy Sobor (St Isaac's Cathedral)

Monument to Imperial self-confidence,
the imposing bulk of St Isaac's Cathedral
rises majestically on the St Petersburg
skyline, its grand dome visible from far
out in the Gulf of Finland.

The cathedral is named after the
patron saint of the Romanov dynasty,
St Isaac of Dalmatia, whose feast day
coincides with Peter the Great's
birthday. Peter was married in the city's
first St Isaac's, a small wooden church
constructed near the Admiralty

(Admiralteystvo). The current cathedral
is the fourth version, begun in 1818 by
order of Alexander I following the
defeat of the French.

Auguste de Montferrand The building
was the life's work of a little-known
French architect, Auguste de
Montferrand (1786–1858). Having
moved to St Petersburg after service in
Napoleon's army, he was the unlikely
winner of the competition to redesign
St Isaac's. His inexperience made him
easy prey to the authoritarian tastes of
Nicholas I expressed in the final
product. The tsar declined his widow's
request that the architect be buried in
the cathedral, but a small bust of
Montferrand, together with his
original models, is on display in
the nave.

Imperial splendour St Isaac's impresses
less by its design than by sheer mass
and wealth of decoration. By the time it
was completed in 1858, construction of
the cathedral over 40 years had
consumed more than 23 million
roubles. Red granite was transported
from Finland for the columns, while
the porticos were topped with dramatic
bronze reliefs. Inside, over 200kg
(440lb) of gold went into gilding, white
marble and lapis lazuli, creating a
unique iconostasis, and the greatest
artists of the day were commissioned to
paint the interior frescos.

Climbing the 262 steps to the
colonnade affords a breathtaking

panorama over St Petersburg's rooftops and the Neva beyond (separate ticket required).
Isaakievskaya Ploshchad 1. Tel: 315 9732. Open: Thur–Tue 10am–7pm (colonnade till 6pm). Admission charge. Metro: Nevskiy Prospekt.

Manezh

The former Horse Guards Riding School was constructed in 1804–7 by the architect Giacomo Quarenghi. On both sides of the portico are sculptures representing the Dioscuri brothers, crafted in marble. They were made in Italy by Paolo Triscorni and delivered in 1817. The building is now the Central Exhibition Hall.

Mariinskiy Dvorets (Mariinskiy Palace)

This palace was built for Nicholas I's daughter Grand Duchess Maria Nikolayevna in 1839–44 by the architect Andrey Stakenschneider. It is now home to the City Legislative Council.

Pamyatnik Nikolaiyu I (Monument to Nicholas I)

Erected facing the cathedral, in the centre of the square in 1856–9, it was designed by the architect Auguste de Montferrand and the sculptor Pyotr Klodt. The equestrian statue has only two points of support.

Siniy Most (The Blue Bridge)

This is the broadest bridge in the city – only 35m (115ft) span but 100m (328ft) wide. The first wooden drawbridge was built in 1737.

Literaturno-Memorialnyi Muzey F M Dostoevskovo (Fyodor Dostoevsky Literary and Memorial Museum)

The original interior of the writer's last apartment is furnished with his

Mariinskiy Palace

The house where Vladimir Nabokov was born and grew up

documents, photographs and personal belongings.
Kuznechny Pereulok 5/2. Tel: 571 4031.
www.md.spb.ru.
Open: Tue–Sun 11am–6pm.
Closed: last Wed of month.
Admission charge.
Metro: Vladimirskaya/Dostoevskaya.

Muzey V V Nabokova (Nabokov Museum)

This is where the famous writer was born and grew up, in a distinctly privileged environment (he was driven to school in the family Rolls-Royce). The author of *Lolita* is commemorated in the personal effects and original furnishings of the house.

Bolshaya Morskaya Ulitsa 47. Tel: 571 4502. www.nabokovmuseum.org.
Open: Tue–Fri 11am–5pm, Sat–Sun noon–5pm. Admission charge.
Metro: Sadovaya.

Muzey Zheleznodorozhnovo Transporta (Museum of Railway Transport)

One of the oldest technical museums in the country, illustrating the history of railway transport in Russia from the beginning. Some machines are still in working order.
Sadovaya Ulitsa 50. Tel: 315 1476.
Open: Wed–Sun 11am–5pm.
Admission charge.
Metro: Sadovaya/Sennaya Ploshchad.

Walk: Neva West Bank to the Griboyedov Canal

The splendours of the Admiralty, the Imperial metropolis, the unnerving haunt of historical spectres ... the district west of Palace Square captures the essence of St Petersburg.

Allow 2 hours.

Start at the Admiralty at the end of Nevskiy Prospekt.

1 Admiralteystvo (The Admiralty)

(*See p98.*)
Walk through the Admiralty garden to Decembrists' Square.

2 Ploshchad Dekabristov (Decembrists' Square)

This square was named after the uprising of Guards officers on 14 December 1825, when troops gathered at the far end of the square to demand constitutional reform. Nicholas I easily crushed the rebellion. The poet Pushkin escaped with a warning, surviving to pen his epic *The Bronze Horseman*, its title taken from the statue of Peter the Great in the square (Medniy Vsadnik).
Turn away from the river and make for St Isaac's Cathedral.

3 Isaakievskaya Ploshchad (St Isaac's Square)

St Isaac's Cathedral gives its name to the impressive square beyond, created in the reign of Nicholas I. Across the 100m (328ft)-wide Blue Bridge, the broadest in the city, Mariinskiy Dvorets (Mariinskiy Palace) dominates the southern end of the square. On the eastern side is the art nouveau Astoria Hotel.
Cross the Moyka River and follow the embankment westwards.

4 Yusupovskiy Dvorets (Yusupov Palace)

This was the residence of Prince Felix Yusupov and the scene of the 1916 assassination of Rasputin, who was poisoned and shot in the head, but refused to die. The terrified conspirators then threw him in the river where he drowned.

The monument to the founder of St Petersburg, Peter the Great

Continue along the embankment and turn left on to Glinki Ulitsa to Theatre Square.

5 Teatralnaya Ploshchad (Theatre Square)

The Mariinskiy Theatre and Rimsky-Korsakov Conservatory were built here in the 19th century. The ballet dancers Anna Pavlova and Vaslav Nijinsky created a sensation at the theatre, while the conservatory nurtured the composers Dmitri Shostakovich and Igor Stravinsky.

Continue along Glinki Ulitsa to St Nicholas's Naval Cathedral.

6 Nikolskiy Morskoi Sobor (St Nicholas's Naval Cathedral)

Standing at the junction of the Kryukov and Griboyedov canals, this was built in 1753–62 in a Baroque style (*see p120*).

Walk back to Nevskiy Prospekt, along either the north or south bank of the Griboyedov Canal or directly along Sadovaya Ulitsa.

Walk: Neva West Bank to the Griboyedov Canal

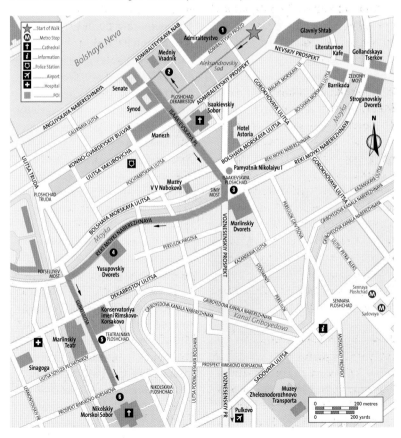

Nikolskiy Morskoi Sobor (St Nicholas's Naval Cathedral)

Designed by Savva Chevakinskiy in the Baroque style, built in 1753–62 for sailors and Admiralty employees, and named after St Nicholas, patron saint of sailors. It contains two churches.
Nikolskaya Ploshchad 1–3.
Metro: Sadovaya/Sennaya Ploshchad.

Sinagoga (Synagogue)

Alexander II authorised construction of the synagogue in 1869. Be prepared to purchase a skullcap on entrance.
Lermontovskiy Prospekt 2.
Metro: Sadovaya/Sennaya Ploshchad.

Sobor Kazanskoi Bogomateri (Cathedral of Our Lady of Kazan)

Built in 1801–11 on the site of a small church that housed the ancient icon of

St Nicholas's Naval Cathedral

Our Lady of Kazan, this is the main Orthodox cathedral and one of the grandest churches in the city.
Kazanskaya Ploshchad 2.
Metro: Nevskiy Prospekt.

Sobor Vladimirskoi Bogomateri (Cathedral of Our Lady of Vladimir)

This was built in 1760–1831 to the designs of Pietro Trezzini and A A Melnikov.
Vladimirskiy Prospekt 20.
Metro: Vladimirskaya/Dostoevskaya.

Stroganovskiy Dvorets (Stroganov Palace)

This Baroque palace (*see map p99*) was designed in 1752–4 by Bartolomeo Rastrelli. The Stroganovs were noted collectors of everything from Egyptian antiquities and Roman coins to icons and old masters.

The building now belongs to the Russian Museum and has a display of porcelain. Also on show here is a collection of waxworks of historical figures.
Nevskiy Prospekt 17. Tel: 312 9054.
Open: Tue–Sun 10am–5pm. Admission charge. Metro: Gostiny Dvor.

PETROGRAD SIDE AND ISLANDS Andreevskiy Sobor (St Andrew's Cathedral)

This Baroque cathedral was built by Alexander Viestt in 1764–80. Andrey Pervozvanniy is the patron saint of Russia, and all ships have flags with his cross. The Order named after him

The cruiser *Aurora* is moored on the Neva River

is the highest award of the Russian Federation.
6-ya Liniya 11.
Metro: Vasileostrovskaya.

Buddiiskiy Khram (Buddhist Temple)

St Petersburg was once well known for its religious tolerance and a prime example of this is the presence of a Buddhist temple, the first to be built in Europe. It belongs to one of Russia's indigenous Buddhist peoples, the Buryats of Eastern Siberia. Although a working place of worship, it bears little resemblance to temples found in Buryatiya, but is still worth a look.
Primorskiy Prospekt 91.
Metro: Staraya Derevnya.

Kreyser *Avrora* (Cruiser *Aurora*)

A blank shot from the cannon of this tiny warship gave the signal for Red Guards to take the Winter Palace in October 1917 (*see pp14–15*), sealing the fate of the Provisional Government and securing the *Aurora* an almost legendary status in Soviet revolutionary history.

The exhibition illustrates the *Aurora*'s participation in the Tsushima battle of the Russo-Japanese War of 1904–5, as well as its role in the October Revolution of 1917 and its participation in World War II.

Floating museum

Today you are free to wander around the immaculately preserved ship, inspect the cannon and take a look at the radio room. A mock-up of sailing conditions – the ship's menu records that Baltic Fleet sailors enjoyed 123g of vodka and salt cabbage daily – is on display below decks. The museum also shows off the red flag that was raised on

the night of the Revolution, as well as period uniforms and weaponry, songs composed in the ship's honour and gifts from various foreign communist dignitaries dating from the heyday of Soviet bloc bonhomie. Today the *Aurora* is maintained by cadets from the nearby Nakhimov Navy School.
Petrovskaya Naberezhnaya 4.
Tel: 230 8440. Open: Tue–Thur, Sat–Sun 10.30am–4pm. Free admission.
Metro: Gorkovskaya.

Mechet (Mosque)

One of Europe's largest and most beautiful mosques, this was opened in 1913 and recently renovated at great expense.

The beautiful Mosque

Kronverkskiy Prospekt.
Metro: Gorkovskaya.

Muzey Antropologii i Etnografii (Museum of Anthropology and Ethnography)

The highlight of this museum is Peter the Great's collection of curiosities, with pickled mutants, both human and animal, that caught the tsar's fancy and for which he paid handsomely.
Kunstkamera, Universitetskaya Naberezhnaya 3. Tel: 328 1412.
www.kunstkamera.ru.
Open: Tue–Sun 11am–6pm.
Closed: last Thur of month.
Admission charge.
Metro: Nevskiy Prospekt/ Vasileostrovskaya.

Muzey Politicheskoi Istorii Rossii (Museum of Political History of Russia)

On display are original objects, documents and photographs showing Russian history of the 19th and 20th centuries including Lenin's office as in July 1917.
Ulitsa Kuybisheva 2/4.
Tel: 233 7052. www.polithistory.ru.
Open: Fri–Wed 10am–6pm.
Admission charge.
Metro: Gorkovskaya.

Petropavlovskaya Krepost (Peter and Paul Fortress)

Designed to protect the Neva lands won from the Swedes during the

PETER THE GREAT
(1672–1725)

Fired by travels abroad in his youth,
Peter modelled his court on Versailles,
streamlined bureaucracy and championed
industrialisation. But despite his passion
for reason in a country steeped in
superstition, Peter had a strong streak of the
barbarian in him. Soirées at the Summer
Palace dissolved into Gothick debauchery.
St Petersburg was constructed, much as
Stalin's projects were, by sheer effort of
will and drastic loss of life. Capable of
extreme cruelty, Peter personally saw to the
torture of Alexei, his only son. Like
Gorbachev, Peter was adored by
Westernisers but was similarly motivated
less by love of the 'effete' West than by
the need to make the Russian system
work better, remarking: 'We shall need
Europe for a few decades and then we can
show her our backside!'

Great Northern War (1700–21), the
founding of the fortress on 16 May
1703 is considered to mark the
establishment of the city itself. It was
first built in wood and later rebuilt
in stone by Domenico Trezzini. One
island was chosen as a construction site,
at the point where the river branches
into three arms: the Bolshaya ('Big')
Neva, Neva and Malaya ('Small') Neva.
The name of the fortress was soon
transferred to the city.

Museums and exhibitions
The Komendantskiy Domik
(Commandant's House) and
Inzhenerniy Korpus (Engineer's
House) display exhibitions of city
history. You can also visit the Nevskaya
Panorama and the Nevskiy Gate.
Across the river from Winter Palace.
Tel: 238 4550.
Open: Thur–Tue 11am–6pm.
Grounds open: daily 6am–10pm.
Metro: Gorkovskaya.

Petropavlovskiy Sobor
(Cathedral of Sts Peter and Paul)
The cathedral is a unique example of
Russian 18th-century architecture and
took 21 years to build. For two
centuries it was the burial place of all
the tsars and grand dukes of Russia,
including Nicholas II, laid to rest in
1998, 80 years after his execution in
Ekaterinburg, a consequence of the
1917 October Revolution and the
collapse of tsarism in Russia.
Open: Thur–Tue 11am–6pm.

Trubetskoi Bastion
From 1872 to 1921 the cells in the
bastion served as a prison. From the
18th century the fortress was a jail
for Russian revolutionaries. Reading
and writing were outlawed and
total isolation was enforced: guards
were forbidden to speak or to
know the identity of inmates and
patrolled soundproofed corridors.
Insubordination meant the *kartser*
or cooler (literally – it was unheated
in winter); mere rudeness to
the guards merited two
days' darkness.
Open: daily 10am–7pm.
Admission charge.

The last of the Romanovs

The unhappy reign of the last of the Romanov dynasty, Tsar Nicholas II, started inauspiciously when 3,000 well-wishers were crushed in the crowd at celebrations marking his coronation in 1896. Later, he gained the nickname 'Bloody Nicholas' after peaceful demonstrators were massacred on Palace Square in 1905. But essentially Nicholas was a timid man.

Devoted to his family and particularly to his sickly, haemophiliac son Alexis, the Emperor and Autocrat of all the Russias was thought by his cousin Kaiser Wilhelm better cut out to be a 'country gentleman growing turnips'. Despite growing civil unrest and mutinies in the fleet, he preferred to spend most of the year at the royal retreat of Tsarskoe Selo.

Meanwhile, his popularly despised German wife Princess Alexandra, granddaughter of Queen Victoria, was besotted with the mystic Rasputin, whom she believed able to cure her son. Society was scandalised: Rasputin's lewd soirées were common knowledge, yet his power over the royal family seemed total. When Rasputin began to advise on appointments to the Duma during World War I, while Nicholas was away at the front, the feeling of unrest increased. Shortly afterwards, Tsar Nicholas's cousin, Grand Duke Dmitri Pavlovich, killed Rasputin, with the help of other family members.

After Rasputin was killed a letter was found forewarning the Romanov family of impending doom:

'I write and leave behind me this letter at St Petersburg. I feel that I shall leave life before January 1 ... If I am killed by common

Tsar Nicholas II, last Emperor of Russia

The Cathedral of Sts Peter and Paul, where the remains of Tsar Nicholas II's family are buried

the family, that is to say, none of your children or relations, will remain alive for more than two years. They will be killed by the Russian people ... You must reflect and act prudently. Think of your safety and tell your relations that I have paid for them with my blood. I shall be killed. I am no longer among the living.'

Finally, the exactions of a deeply unpopular war brought Russia to boiling point. Huge food riots rampaged through Petrograd. The army had revolted. Nicholas signed his abdication in a railway carriage in pencil as 'others do when they make a list of dirty laundry'. On 2 March 1917, tsarism died.

Its resting place was to be a mineshaft near Ekaterinburg in the Urals where, in July the following year, Nicholas, his family, servants and the pet spaniel were shot, doused in sulphuric acid and dumped by Bolshevik secret police. The final order to blow up even the building where the murders were committed was given in 1977 by the then local Party chief, Boris Yeltsin.

But it was Yeltsin who promoted the reburial of the rediscovered remains in 1998, in St Petersburg's Cathedral of Sts Peter and Paul (*see p123*) – despite the opposition of the Orthodox Church.

assassins, and especially by my brothers the Russian peasants, you, Tsar of Russia, have nothing to fear, remain on your throne and govern, and you, Russian Tsar, will have nothing to fear for your children, they will reign for hundreds of years in Russia ... if it was your relations who have wrought my death, then no one in

Walk: Basil Island and the Spit

The majestic view of the Neva delta from the spit of Basil (Vasilevskiy) Island readily conjures up the dream of maritime grandeur that obsessed Peter the Great. Embracing some of the city's oldest buildings, the island's streets still evoke the breathtaking Imperial self-confidence that fired the tsar's vision.

Allow 2 hours, excluding museum visits.

Start at Vasileostrovskaya metro station. Turn right down 6 and 7 Lines (Linii).

1 To Bolshoi Prospekt
Make for the pink bell tower of the Andreevskiy Sobor (Cathedral of St Andrew) of 1780.

Turning left along leafy Bolshoi Prospekt, note No 6 where Tatyana Savicheva, whose diary is exhibited at the Piskaryovskoe Cemetery, recorded the starvation of her family during the Siege. The 1771 Lyuteranskaya Tserkov Svaytoi Ekateriny (Lutheran Church of St Catherine) stands opposite.
Turn right on to 1 Line (liniya), passing to the left the former Imperial Cadet barracks, site of Lenin's first bid for power at the Soviet of Workers' and Soldiers' Deputies in June 1917. At the river turn left on to Universitetskaya Naberezhnaya.

2 Menshikovskiy Dvorets (Menshikov Palace)
Ochre paintwork and Dutch-style gables characterise the palace built from 1710 to 1720 for Peter's friend and favourite Alexander Menshikov (1673–1729), first governor of the city.

The rooms have been carefully restored, the highlights being the tiled first-floor quarters, the lathe at which Peter amused himself, and the kitchen's enormous wooden beer vessel. Menshikov's luck turned after the deaths of Peter and his wife (Menshikov's former mistress) Catherine I, and he died in Siberian exile, penniless.

The palace is now a branch of the Hermitage, with an exhibition on Russian culture from 1700 to the 1730s. *Tel: 323 1112. www.hermitagemuseum. org. Open: Tue–Sun. Admission charge. Tours: 10.30am–4.30pm.*
Continue up Universitetskaya Nabereznaya.

3 Zdaniye Dvenadtsati Kollegiy (The Twelve Colleges Building)
Among St Petersburg's oldest buildings, they were built for Peter's bureaucracy. Given to the university

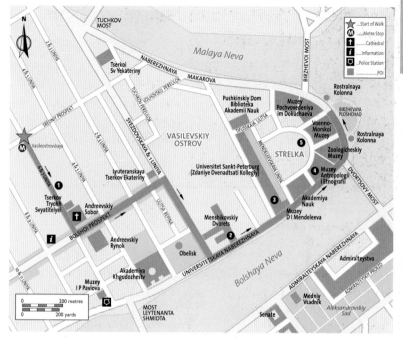

in 1819, they became an epicentre of militancy. Lenin graduated from the law faculty, but soon abandoned his legal career to devote himself to Marxism and the struggle towards a socialist revolution.

Continue along the embankment.

4 Muzey Antropologii i Etnografii (Museum of Anthropology and Ethnography)

This museum is also known as the Kunstkamera. Peter's fascination with science led him during a trip to Holland to purchase the collection of anatomical oddities at the heart of Russia's first museum (1718). Free vodka enticed visitors to gaze at

pickled, bottled freaks that, over 250 years on, have lost none of their power to shock (*see p122*).

Return to the embankment passing the Zoological Museum (see p129).

5 Strelka (The Spit)

Commanding a superb view of the Peter and Paul Fortress and the Winter Palace, the Strelka – or island spit – is a St Petersburg symbol.

The Stock Exchange, now the Voenno-Morskoi Muzey (Naval Museum – *see p129*), dominates the Strelka, flanked by former warehouses and the defunct Customs House, mute witnesses to the commercial hubbub once focused here.

St Petersburg

One of the rostral columns on the Spit, Basil Island

The Spit of Basil Island

Sampsonievskiy Sobor (Sampsonievskiy Cathedral)

This Baroque cathedral, now set amid an industrial landscape, is said to have been the place Catherine the Great married her lover Grigory Potemkin in 1774. It also possesses St Petersburg's heaviest bell and a wonderfully elaborate Orthodox interior.

Bolshaya Sampsonievskiy Prospekt 41.
Tel: 315 4361. Free admission.
Metro: Vyborgskaya.

Tsentralniy Voenno-Morskoi Muzey (Central Naval Museum)

Located in the historical premises of the former Stock Exchange, this is the world's largest naval museum, founded in 1708. It has over 800,000 items, including dioramas and intricate models of ships of the Russian fleet. Do not miss Peter the Great's *botik,* the tiny rowing boat, also known as the 'Grandfather of the Russian Navy', in which Peter the Great learnt to sail.

Birzhevaya Ploshchad 4.
Tel: 328 2501.
www.museum.navy.ru.
Open: Wed–Sun 11am–6pm.
Closed: last Thur of month.
Admission charge.
Metro: Nevskiy Prospekt/
Vasileostrovskaya.

Voenno-Istoricheskiy Muzey Artillerii, Inzhenernyh Voysk i Voysk Svyazi (Military-Historical Museum of Artillery, Engineers and Signal Corps)

Housed in the old Arsenal is the world's largest military museum, founded in 1703, with over 750,000 items including armaments, uniforms, banners, orders and battle relics. An open-air display features a variety of weaponry.

Alexandrovskiy Park 7.
Tel: 238 4704. Open: Wed–Sun
11am–5pm. Closed: last Thur of month.
Admission charge.
Metro: Gorkovskaya.

Zoologicheskiy Muzey (Zoological Museum)

With over 17 million species, 500,000 of them on display, the museum is one of the finest of its kind in the world. The exhibits include a set of stuffed animals and a world-famous collection of mammoths.

Universitetskaya Naberezhnaya 1.
Tel: 328 0112. Open: Sat–Thur
11am–6pm. Admission charge.
Metro: Nevskiy Prospekt/
Vasileostrovskaya.

Excursions from St Petersburg

St Petersburg is surrounded by a necklace of world-famous suburbs, most of them former residences of the emperors. It is impossible to come to St Petersburg and not admire the palaces and parks, architectural gems in their own rights. Further afield, Kizhi Island and Tsarskoe Selo are unmissable experiences.

Gatchina

In 1765 Catherine the Great presented this village to her lover Prince Orlov, who commissioned Antonio Rinaldi to build a neoclassical palace, which was completed in 1781.
Krasnoarmeyskiy Prospekt 1, Gatchina, Leningrad Region. Tel: 13492. Open: Tue–Sun 10am–6pm. Closed: first Tue of month. Take suburban train from the Baltiysky terminus, or bus K18 from Moskovskiy railway station.

Kronstadt

This sea-fortress and port has over 300 historic structures, including extensive fortifications and a cathedral.
Take bus 510/510-E from Staraya Derevnya metro station to Kronstadt. In summer, the hydrofoil-vessel Meteor runs from the quay near Tuchkov Bridge to Kronstadt quay.

Lake Ladoga – Valaam

In the northern part of Lake Ladoga lie Valaam Island and about 50 smaller ones. Valaam is one of Russia's most ancient and important monasteries. *Difficult to reach. Contact tourist information or local travel agencies for more details (see p189). Further details about the monastery can be found at: www.valaam.ru*

Lake Onega – Kizhi

This peaceful island serves as a museum of 18th-century wooden architecture. The Cathedral of the Transfiguration has 22 unpainted wooden domes.
There are hydrofoils over Lake Onega to Kizhi; operate from Petrozavodsk end of May to end of Sept.

Oranienbaum (Lomonosov)

Prince Menshikov began a palace and park in the early 18th century. The future Peter III then built a palace. The entire complex has been undergoing renovation in recent years.
Dvortsovy Prospekt 48, Lomonosov. Tel: 422 4796/423 1641. Open: Wed–Sun 10am–5pm, Mon 11am–5pm.

Admission charge. Take suburban train from the Baltiysky terminus.

Pavlovsk
Catherine the Great presented this palace to her son, Grand Duke Paul, in 1777.
Ulitsa Revolutsii 20, Pavlovsk. Tel: 812 425 1214. www.pavlovskmuseum.ru. Open: Sat–Thur 10am–5pm. Admission charge. Take suburban train from Vitebsky terminus.

Peterhof (Petrodvorets)
In 1704 Peter I built a wooden house here so he could oversee the construction of the island fortress of Kronstadt. The palace, built in 1713–23, was later extended.

Bolshoi Dvorets (Grand Palace)
Filled with lavish rooms and galleries, this dominates the estate, which also contains 144 fountains.
Razvodnaya Ulitsa 2. Tel: 427 0073. www.peterhof.ru. Open: Tue–Sun 10.30am–6pm. Closed: last Tue of month. Admission charge. Take suburban train from the Baltiysky terminus, or bus.

Tsarskoe Selo (Pushkin)
Peter the Great regained this place, 24km (15 miles) south of St Petersburg, from Sweden. It was the first town with electricity in Europe.
www.tzar.ru.

Take suburban train from the Vitebsky terminus, or coach.

Aleksandrovskiy Dvorets (Alexander Palace)
Built in the late 18th century for Alexander I.
Dvortsovaya Ulitsa 2, Tsarskoe Selo. Tel: 466 6071. www.alexanderpalace.org/palace. Open: Wed–Mon 10am–5pm. Closed: last Wed of month. Admission charge.

Ekaterinskiy Dvorets (Catherine Palace)
Tsarskoe Selo's oldest building, this was rebuilt in 1752 by Rastrelli for Tsarina Elizabeth, who named it after her mother, Catherine I.
Sadovaya Ulitsa 7, Tsarskoe Selo. Tel: 465 5308. Open: Wed–Mon 10am–5pm. Closed: last Mon of month. Admission charge.

Litsey (Lyceum)
Pushkin's presence can be felt in the Lyceum, where he went to school.
Sadovaya Ulitsa 2, Tsarskoe Selo. Tel: 476 6411. Open: Wed–Mon 10.30am–5pm. Closed: last Mon of month. Admission charge.

Velikiy Novgorod
Russia's oldest town, founded in 862. At its heart is the Cathedral of St Sophia built in 1045.
Tourist office tel: 816 277 3074. www.visitnovgorod.ru. Take suburban train from the Moskovskiy terminal, or coach.

Getting away from it all

Even the most hardened sightseer is likely to tire of the hectic pace, frantic crowds and traffic fumes of Moscow and St Petersburg. Fortunately, both cities offer a variety of means of escape; they may sometimes involve a little travelling, but the results are worth it. The following entries are just a few of the many excursions on offer.

MOSCOW
Arkhangelskoe

Prince Golitsyn's magnificent country house is the highlight of this beautiful spot just outside the city. The house was built of stucco-covered timber by Rastrelli, architect of St Petersburg's Winter Palace, and is luxuriously appointed with tapestries and 18th-century furniture. The estate's landscaped gardens lead down to the Moskva River in a series of terraces.
Krasnogorsk Region. Tel: 495 363 1375. www.arkhangelskoe.ru. Open: Wed–Sun 10.30am–4.30pm. Admission charge. Metro: Tushinskaya, then bus 549 to Arkhangelskoe stop.

Boulevards and parks

You need not travel far to escape Moscow's urban intensity – a stroll along the ring of boulevards in the town centre is often enough to restore a little sanity. Tverskoi, Gogolevskiy and Rozhdestvenskiy Boulevards are among the best for people-watching, as old men argue over chessboards in summer and fur-coated toddlers are taken for sledge rides in winter. Alternatively, head for the forested parks on the outskirts of town. Izmaylovskiy Park and Bittsa Forest are two of the best.
Metro: Izmaylovskiy Park/Bittsevskiy Park.

Bukhta Radosti (Bay of Joys)

Half an hour's hydrofoil (*raketa*) ride from the river boat terminal at **Rechnoi Vokzal** metro brings you to the 'Bay of Joys', a popular riverside picnic spot in the warmer months. Stock up with a loaf of black bread, sausage, pickled herrings, cheese and a bottle of Moldovan red wine.
Phone the Moscow River Boat Company for departure and last return times. Leningradskoye Shosse 59. Tel: 363 9628. www.rechflot.ru (Russian only). Metro: Rechnoi Vokzal.

Kolomenskoe

Peter the Great spent much of his childhood at this ancient and picturesque estate on the Moskva River. Originally a 14th-century village of artisans and fishermen, its commanding location made it a strategic point in Muscovy's seemingly ceaseless battles. Dmitri Donskoi massed his troops on the hill before the decisive battle of Kulikovo in 1380. Ivan the Terrible made it the first stage of his campaign to capture the Tartar stronghold of Kazan. Many of the wizened oak trees still standing were even then already several centuries old.

Today the site is an open-air museum, **Muzey-Zapovednik XVI–XVII vi 'Kolomenskoe'**. The rugged beauty of the 1532 **Church of the Ascension** is the chief attraction, closely followed by the azure cupolas of the **Church of Our Lady of Kazan** visible through the estate gateway. A number of unique wooden buildings were transferred to the estate in the 1930s, including the simple log cabin from which Peter directed his northern campaigns, a defence tower from the White Sea and a 17th-century mead distillery from the nearby village of Preobrazhenskoye.

A great place for sledging and cross-country skiing in winter, Kolomenskoe is at its most enchanting as the sun sets and a largely elderly congregation gathers for evening prayers at the Kazan Church.

Andropova Prospekt 39. Tel: 499 615 2768. Grounds open year round.
Buildings open: Tue–Sun 10am–5pm.
Admission charge for the small decorative arts museum. Metro: Kolomenskaya, then follow the signs to the estate.

Kuntsevo

The woodlands on the steep river banks between Kuntsevskaya and Bagrationovskaya metro stations are ideal for a summer picnic or for tobogganing in winter. On a clear day in autumn, the view across the river

A tree-lined pathway invites a quiet stroll

through the orange and crimson sycamore trees is stunning.

Metro: Kuntsevskaya. Exit on to Malaya Filyovskaya Ulitsa, walk 300m (330yds) back towards the centre and cut up through the apartment blocks to the woodlands beyond.

Kuskovo

On the outskirts of Moscow, the Kuskovo estate is a wonderful escape from the city. It was built in the 18th century for Count Sheremetev (*see pp80–81*), owner of over a million

The Orangery at Kuskovo is now a ceramics museum

hectares (4,000sq miles) of land. Although ravaged by Napoleon's troops in 1812, a fine ensemble of Russian architecture remains, surrounded by a landscaped park and lake.

The two-storey wooden palace, once the scene of Sheremetev's lavish society balls, retains its opulent interior decoration and forms part of a museum of ceramics on the estate, made up of private collections nationalised after the Revolution.

The estate is also the setting for a summer season of evening concerts – check listings in the press.

Ulitsa Yunosti 2. Tel: 495 370 0160. Open: summer Wed–Sun 10am–6pm; winter Wed–Sun 10am–4pm. Closed: last Wed of month. Admission charge. Metro: Ryazanskiy Prospekt, then bus 133 or 208 six stops.

Serebryaniy Bor ('Silver Pine Forest')

This secluded island on the Moskva River is a favourite destination of Muscovites on hot summer weekends. Communist Party officials built the many exclusive dachas here, now being bought up by the capital's new ruling class of businessmen because of the relatively clean location upstream of heavy industry. For those not tempted to swim, the island is a great place to indulge the Russian passion for mushrooms and berry picking.

Take trolleybus 21 from Polezhayevskaya metro along Prospekt Marshala Zhukova right on to the island.

The entrance to Tsaritsyno estate

Tsaritsyno

Surrounded by forested parks and ornamental lakes, the picturesque ruins at Tsaritsyno in the south of the city are all that remain of one of Moscow's strangest royal retreats. It was designed in red brick and limestone by Vasili Bazhenov, in a peculiar cocktail of architectural styles, for Catherine the Great. Visiting Moscow in 1787, Catherine was appalled by Tsaritsyno, reportedly describing the turret pavilions as akin to candles around a coffin. With wars against the Turks consuming ever more of the Imperial budget, Tsaritsyno was never completed. The park's ornamental bridges and several of the estate's buildings, including Bazhenov's Opera House, have been undergoing restoration. Boats can be hired on the lakes in summer.

Access to the grounds is free. Tsaritsyno Palace. Tel: 495 355 4844. Open: Wed–Fri 11am–5pm, Sat–Sun 11am–7pm. Admission charge. Metro: Tsaritsyno. Leave the station from the exit nearer the front of the train, head under the railway bridges, take the right fork, turning left at the lakes to the estate entrance.

Russian winter

A time of picturesque charm and long, cold nights; of festivities; of perilous streets and treacherous pavements ... winter is the quintessential Russian experience.

The first frosts set in at the end of *babye lyeto* – 'woman's summer' – a brief spell of warmer weather in autumn compared to the last flowering of female beauty before old age. Apart from occasional short-lived thaws, the winter in Moscow and St Petersburg lasts through to early March and the festival of Maslenitsa, its pagan origins alive in the roaring bonfires and orgiastic consumption of vodka and the soured-cream-doused pancakes – *blini* – that symbolise the sun.

On 31 December Russian children sleep restlessly in anticipation of what Ded-Moroz – 'Grandfather Frost' – and his girl helper Snegurochka will bring for Novy God – New Year – still the biggest Russian holiday.

On a more mundane level, the all-encompassing *slyakot* – a singularly Russian mixture of mud, slush and

The snowy Kronverk Embankment near the Peter and Paul Fortress in St Petersburg

The frozen seaside at Peterhof

the iced paths of Gorky Park, and an army of the tracksuited elderly cruising the woods on cross-country skis. Strangest of all are the ice swimmers, nicknamed *morzh* ('walruses'), whose favourite pastime in a heavy frost is to strip down and plunge into gaps in the ice before setting off on a barefooted jog across the snow.

Russian people are used to winter and Moscow's location makes even very low temperatures more bearable than anywhere else. Even so, be prepared that during occasional severe conditions you might be stuck indoors for a couple of days. You might be forced to take short walks, hopping from sight to sight, or follow the Russian example of hopping from one vodka stall to another.

sleet that accompanies the thaw – means going out armed with a change of shoes. Everybody wears furs, but note: hell hath no fury like a cloakroom attendant who discovers your coat is missing the loop for hanging. Similarly, *babushkas* verbally lambast mothers on the street whose children they consider inadequately dressed.

Since 988, when Prince Vladimir of Kiev rejected Islam in favour of Christianity (because the former's condemnation of alcohol was unsuitable to the Russian climate), the colder months have been the occasion for increased drinking, and each winter brings its toll of deaths by frostbite of those who were reckless enough to stop for a snooze on the way home from a boisterous night out.

Snow and ice bring out tobogganing children, couples skating

Time to show off new fur hats or coats

ST PETERSBURG
Finskiy Zaliv (Gulf of Finland)

Three capital cities – St Petersburg, Tallinn and Helsinki – stand on the Gulf of Finland. If you have time for a paddle in summer or a walk on the ice in winter, its north shore has sandy beaches and shaded woodland where many citizens have their summer dachas. Slightly inland, Lake Razliv is a favourite picnic spot near the town of Sestroretsk (34km/21 miles). Further up the coast is the village of Repino (50km/31 miles), named after the painter Ilya Repin, whose estate is now a museum.

Museum I E Repin

Visitors can see the artist's study, dining room and studio. The grounds and setting are extremely picturesque.

Primorskoe Shosse 411. Tel: 812 432 0828. Open: Wed–Mon 10.30am–5pm. Admission charge.
How to get there: suburban train from the Finland terminus (for the coast, pick one going to Sestroretsk and get off at any attractive spot; for Repino, any train headed for Zelenogorsk); or taxi-bus along Primorskoe Shosse, the coast road.

Griboyedov Canal

Without leaving the city centre, a stroll along the banks of the former Catherine Canal is a good way to unwind. Starting at Nevskiy Prospekt, pass the Cathedral of Our Lady of Kazan, and walk up to Kryukov Canal towards New Holland (Novaya Gollandiya) island. This island, once

The Gulf of Finland

Interior room at Elagin Palace

used for storing ship timber, was named after the Dutch shipbuilders who inspired Peter the Great. You can join boat tours from Nevskiy Prospekt, on the Griboyedov Canal, Fontanka River or Moyka River.

Kirov Islands

If you wish to escape the city, Elagin Island is for you. The palace grounds, now the Central Park of Culture and Rest (famous for its water attractions), make up most of the island. Its centrepiece is the Elagin Palace, built in 1822 for the mother of Tsar Alexander I. In summer, you can hire boats here or take a cruise on the Gulf of Finland. Kamenniy (Stone) is the island of recreation and relaxation, boasting many historic aristocratic mansions and also an 18th-century palace, built by Catherine the Great for her son, Paul.
Metro: Chernaya Rechka.

Krestovskiy Island is best known for its sports stadium, but is also an attractive area for walking.
Metro: Krestovskiy Ostrov.

Urn on the steps at Elagin Palace

Shopping

Nowadays shopping, in Moscow and St Petersburg at least, is no longer the nightmarish experience it once was. On the contrary, if you have the money you can buy just about anything you might need on your trip or as a souvenir – everything from lacquerware and ceramics to vodka and CDs. When shopping in the souvenir markets be sure to compare prices as there are plenty of hustlers and conmen about. However, don't expect great value for money.

HOW TO SHOP

When embarking on a shopping spree, you should remember that there are broadly two kinds of store in Russia.

The Western-managed shops function just as you would expect and may accept credit cards. Sales assistants often speak English. Even if they do not, they will be relatively attentive and helpful.

In the former state stores expect to queue to see the goods, queue to pay for them and then queue to hand over the receipt and receive your purchase. Sales assistants are still extraordinarily rude, despite a decree by the Moscow mayor that shopkeepers are obliged to be nice to customers! Do not stand on ceremony – if you wait to be noticed, you will not leave the shop before nightfall. Lastly, do not forget to bring your own bag since few Russian shops provide them.

SOUVENIRS

Amber, gold, furs, lacquerware, glossy art books, CDs, caviar, vodka and domestic brandies and 'champagne' are all good value in Russia. (Remember customs regulations, however – *see p180*.)

The market in Soviet memorabilia is stronger than ever. Ironic 'Leninist' T-shirts, Soviet-era bric-a-brac and odd items of military apparel – you'll find them all in the tourist flea markets. Bear in mind, though, that old uniforms and army belts are unlikely to be originals. More traditional favourites are gaudily painted mugs, plates and spoons from the village of Khokhloma outside Moscow, 'Matryoshka' stacking dolls and elaborately lacquered boxes (*palekh*). Fake versions of all these will be earnestly offered to you at the markets; to be safe, it is advisable to confine serious purchases to specialist souvenir shops, where the more you pay the better your chances of obtaining the real thing.

The Moscow haven for souvenir hunters is the **Izmaylovskiy Market**, open at weekends and selling everything from fighter pilots' helmets and stolen icons to handmade jewellery

and traditional costumes. Bargain hard (but *see* Customs, *p180*).
Turn left out of Izmaylovskiy Park metro and pass the high-rise hotel complex. The market gates are in front of you.

The equivalent in St Petersburg is **Klenovaya Alleya**, open daily in the season.
From Gostiny Dvor metro, head towards Ploshchad Iskusstv and turn right along Inzhenernaya Ulitsa.

Both cities also have open-air art bazaars selling local contemporary work. The main centre in Moscow is opposite the entrance to Gorky Park (*metro: Park Kultury*), in St Petersburg along Nevskiy Prospekt.

Moscow's souvenir shops include **Yantar** (*All Russia Exhibition Centre, No 66 (Cultural Pavilion). Metro: VDNKh*), which specialises in amber jewellery, chessboards, mosaics, etc.
Arbatskaya Lavitsa (*Arbat 27. Tel: 495 290 5689. Open: daily 9am–9pm*) stocks a huge range of souvenirs from across Russia.

In St Petersburg try the **Lomonosov Porcelain Factory outlet** (*Prospekt Obukhovskoi Oboroniy 151. Tel: 812 326 1744. Metro: Lomonovskaya*), where you can pick up exquisite pieces from one of Europe's oldest porcelain producers for a reasonable price. **Passazh** (*Nevskiy Prospekt 48. Metro: Nevskiy Prospekt/ Gostiny Dvor*): several shops in this beautiful late 19th-century shopping centre sell good-quality porcelain, glassware and antiques as well as other souvenirs.

A selection of 'Matryoshka' dolls

BOOKS
Useful bookshops in Moscow include **Biblio-Globus** (*Myasnitskaya Ulitsa 6. Tel: 495 628 3567. www.biblio-globus.ru. Metro: Lubyanka*), **Anglia British Bookshop** (*Vorotnikovsky Pereulok 6/11. Tel: 495 299 7766*) and **Dom Inostrannoy Knigi** (*Kuznetskiy Most 18/7. Tel: 495 628 2021*).

Bookworms in St Petersburg can visit **Dom Knigi** (House of Books), the largest bookstore in the city with books in numerous languages.
28 Nevskiy Prospekt. Tel: 448 2355. Metro: Nevskiy Prospekt/Gostiny Dvor.

CAVIAR AND COGNAC
Once widely available and relatively cheap, black Beluga caviar is now in short supply thanks to the endangered status of Caspian Sea sturgeon from which it is taken. Buy only from authorised dealers; if you source caviar on the black market, you are probably

breaking the law and may end up with an expensive tin of ball bearings in axle grease for your troubles.

Locally produced drinks have all but disappeared from the streets under the deluge of imported beverages, but are nevertheless worth seeking out. Armenian *konyak* (brandy) is highly thought of outside the former USSR, as are Georgian and Crimean wines, though the former are now hard to come by since the war in 2008 between Russia and its neighbour. Another fine souvenir is real Russian Smirnovskaya vodka, recognisable by its tapering bottle. Try the following outlets:

Moscow:
Globus Gourmet

This temple to victuals from around the world is a gourmet's heaven with every kind of Russian speciality sitting side by side with Spanish ham, English tea and French wine.

Prospekt Engelsa 33. Metro: Udelnaya.

Yelisevsky

This exquisite deli is reminiscent of the food hall at Harrods.

Tverskaya Ulitsa 14. Metro: Pushkinskaya/Tverskaya.

DEPARTMENT STORES
Moscow:
Gosudarstvenny Universalniy Magazin (GUM)

Moscow's chief department store translates in typical Soviet style as State Department Store, and is better known as GUM (pronounced 'goom'). The impressive building's vast glass canopy covers galleried shops within, once packed only with shoddy electrical devices, outsize bras and queues. Now privatised, it is a mall to rival Paris's best. Europe's classiest boutiques have now replaced the old state shops.

Krasnaya Ploshchad 3. Tel: 495 788 4343. www.gum.ru. Open: daily 10am–10pm. Metro: Ploshchad Revolyutsii.

Petrovskiy Passazh

Petrovka Ulitsa 10. Metro: Teatralnaya.

TsUM

Ulitsa Petrovka 2. Tel: 495 933 7300. www.tsum.ru. Open: Mon–Sat 10am–10pm, Sun 11am–10pm. Metro: Teatralnaya.

St Petersburg:
Gostiny Dvor complex

Nevskiy Prospekt 35. Metro: Gostiny Dvor.

Passazh

Nevskiy Prospekt 48. Metro: Nevskiy Prospekt/Gostiny Dvor.

FURS

A lot of furs on sale are Scandinavian, so ask if you want the Russian article.

Moscow:
Snegovik

Prospekt Mira 89. Tel: 495 616 2126. Metro: Alekseyevskaya.

Many other branches across the city.

Snezhnaya Koroleva

Bargains galore at this branch of a popular chain.

Shelkovskoye Shosse 1. Tel: 495 777 8999. Metro: Cherkizovskaya.

Several shops in the GUM arcade on Red Square also sell furs.

St Petersburg:
Lena
Nevskiy Prospekt 50. Tel: 907 1047.
www.lenafur.ru.
Metro: Nevskiy Prospekt.

SHOPPING CENTRES
(*See also* Department Stores)
Moscow:
Evropeysky
Huge Western-style shopping mall with many high-street names, cafés, bars and restaurants.
Kievskaya Ploshchad 2.
Metro: Kievskaya.
Okhotny Ryad
Manezhnaya Ploshchad 1.
Tel: 495 737 8449.
Metro: Okhotny Ryad.

St Petersburg:
Varshavskiy Express
Shopping complex over three levels, with many familiar brands.
Obvodnovo Naberezhnaya 118.
www.we.tkspb.ru.
Metro: Baltiyskaya.

SPORTS SUPPLIES
Moscow:
Sportmaster
Skates, skis, rucksacks, clothing, trainers, etc. are available from this chain.
Sadovaya Bolshaya 1. Tel: 495 777 7771.
www.sportmaster.ru. Metro:
Mayakovskaya.

St Petersburg:
Bosco Sport
High-end sports emporium.
Nevskiy Prospekt 54. Tel: 633 3358.
Metro: Nevskiy Prospekt.

SUPERMARKETS
Both cities are dotted with foreign-run supermarkets that sell a wide range of food, toiletries, etc. Prices are higher than in most European countries.
Moscow:
Armeniya
Food from Russia and the Caucasus.
Tverskaya Ulitsa 17. Tel: 495 629 1954.
Metro: Tverskaya.
Azbuka Vkusa
Supermarket chain with stores across the Russian capital.
Prospekt Mira 58. Tel: 495 504 3478.
Metro: Prospekt Mira.
Ramstore
Ulitsa Komsomolskaya 6.
www.ramstore.ru.
Metro: Komsomolskaya. Open: 24/7.
Seventh Continent
Another multi-store Moscow chain with international brands.
Ulitsa Lubyanka Bolshaya, 12.
Tel: 495 777 7779.
Metro: Kuznetskiy Most.

St Petersburg:
Prisma
Brand new supermarket in the basement of the Moscow Hotel Centre.
Ploshchad Aleksandra Nevskovo 2.
Metro: Ploshchad Aleksandra Nevskovo.

The market

The market – *rynok* – is a central element of city life in Moscow and St Petersburg. Somehow, these strongholds of small-scale capitalism managed to survive communism's assault on private property. This was not least, perhaps, because even the most dutiful party functionary relied on the markets for that little something special when the shelves of the state shops were barren of all but a few wizened beetroot and dusty jars of pickled cucumbers.

Moscow's Cheryomushinskiy or St Petersburg's Kuznechniy markets are an experience in themselves, a microcosm of the old Soviet Union. Traders from all corners of the former empire accost the casual visitor: swarthy Georgians proffer bright red roses 'for the beautiful lady, sir'; Uzbeks and Turkmen crouch over piles of watermelons and sacks of roasted sunflower seeds; buxom Ukrainians invite you to try their national favourite – huge slabs of pork fat

Fresh vegetables at a St Petersburg market

Spend some time enjoying the sights and sounds of Kuznechniy market

called *salo*; fishermen from the Caspian Sea stand proudly in front of bucketfuls of red (though no longer black) caviar; and old ladies in bright headscarves sell salted tomatoes and pickled garlic from their allotments in the suburbs of the city.

Some of the goods are as exotic as the salespeople, ranging from fish from Lake Baikal to Armenian brandies and *kvas*, Russia's traditional black bread 'beer'. The meat section is not for the squeamish, with cuts that have long disappeared from Western supermarkets – pigs' trotters, goats' heads, complete ox tongues and internal organs best left unnamed. And, for refreshment, there is sure to be a bottle of the country's lethal moonshine, *samogon*, discreetly hidden under the counter.

The welcome is warm and the sales patter persuasive. Little has changed since the 19th century when a foreign traveller noted that the stallholders in Russia's markets have, 'notwithstanding their lust of gain, a cheerfulness of temperament wholly wanting to the German or the English merchant'.

Entertainment

No trip to Russia is quite complete without an evening at the legendary Bolshoi Theatre in Moscow or St Petersburg's world-famous Mariinskiy Theatre, still sometimes known by its Soviet name, the Kirov. But as befits one of the world's great cultures, entertainment possibilities are virtually endless and there is sure to be something to suit everyone.

What's on

Planning your time amid the wealth of entertainment on offer is probably the greatest problem for culture-hungry visitors to Russia. Members of package tours may find that a trip to the Bolshoi or Mariinskiy is already included in their schedule, simplifying the decision-making process. Otherwise, the best sources of information are the various entertainments listings.

Most convenient are the inserts printed periodically in the English-language newspapers distributed free of charge in Western-style hotels, bars and foreign-run supermarkets. The *Moscow Times* (*www.themoscowtimes.com*) publishes exhaustive listings in their pages every Friday. The former also prints on the back page a short daily 'What is to be done?' column listing the evening's highlights. Similar listings are available for St Petersburg in *Pulse* magazine (*www.pulse.ru*) and the *St Petersburg Times* (*www.sptimes.ru*).

Most hotels have a service bureau that will inform you of current events or group trips organised by local tour agencies or by the hotel itself.

Tickets

The best way of obtaining tickets is to contact one of the agencies mentioned below. Alternatively, try the service bureaux in the hotels, but give them as much notice as possible as tickets sell out quickly. Where major venues are concerned, a two-tier pricing policy operates to ensure that Westerners pay inflated prices. While it is theoretically possible to buy face-value tickets at box offices, you will find it virtually impossible to get into the venue unless you can pass as a Russian.

TICKET AGENCIES
Moscow:

Kassir
Tel: 495 730 7300. www.kassir.ru
Kontramarka
Tel: 495 933 3200. www.kontramarka.ru

St Petersburg:
Mariinskiy Ticket Office
Gostiny Dvor Branch. Tel: 326 4141.
www.mariinsky.ru
Sofit
All tickets.
Vladimirskiy Prospekt 19.
Tel: 327 7400.
www.sofit.spb.ru
Vizit
For ballet performances in the
Aleksandrinskiy Theatre.
Italianskaya 10. Tel: 314 0644.

CINEMAS
Moscow:
35mm
Non-stop shows of European, Asian
and American alternative films.
Pokrovka 47/24. Tel: 495 917 1883.
Metro: Kurskaya/Krasnye Vorota.
Dome Cinema
A plush cinema offering the latest
releases in their original language.
Olympiyskiy Prospekt 18. Tel: 495 931
9873. www.domecinema.ru.
Metro: Prospekt Mira.
Gorizont (Horizon)
A-list films and comfortable seats.
Komsomolskiy Prospekt 21/10.
Tel: 495 795 3795. Metro: Frunzenskaya.
Illyuzion (Illusion)
Large cinema.
Prospekt 100 Let Vadivostoku 103.
Tel: 495 406 406. www.illuzion.ru.
Metro: Taganskaya.
Pushkinskiy (Pushkin's Cinema)
Very large cinema with a huge screen.
Pushkinskaya Ploshchad 2.

Tel: 495 545 0505.
Metro: Pushkinskaya.

St Petersburg:
Aurora Cinema
A swish cinema housed in a beautiful
neoclassical building.
Nevskiy Prospekt 60. Tel: 315 5254.
www.avrora.spb.ru. Metro: Gostiny
Dvor/Nevskiy Prospekt.
Crystal Palace
Another elegant picture house with
four floors.
Nevskiy Prospekt 72. Tel: 272 2382.
www.cp.spb.ru. Metro: Vladimirskaya/
Dostoyevskaya.
Dom Kino
Dating from 1917, this is another long-
time favourite.
Ulitsa Karavannaya 12. Tel: 314 5614.
www.domkino.spb.ru. Metro: Gostiny
Dvor/Nevskiy Prospekt.
Mirazh (Mirage) Cinema
Four-screen theatre; tickets can be
booked online.
Bolshoi Prospekt, Petrogradskaya side 35.
Tel: 235 4911. www.mirage.ru. Metro:
Chkalovskaya.

CLUBS AND CASINOS
Russia's *nouveaux riches* either make
their money or spend it at the profusion
of nightclubs and casinos whose neon
lights illuminate the main streets of
Moscow and St Petersburg after dark.

More tasteful than their Soviet-era
counterparts, they often boast fashion
shows, restaurants and Western DJs in
addition to the dancing and gaming.

Entertainment

They can be a little disconcerting for the uninitiated. Be prepared to be thoroughly searched for firearms by beefy guards on entry. Some charge a hefty entrance fee and nearly all demand a reasonable standard of dress (jacket and tie for men).

The quality and safety of any of the places mentioned below can vary drastically in a short time, depending on whether or not it has been adopted by one of the local mafia groups.

When you leave, you will find that taxis are a lot cheaper if you walk just a few blocks away from the club entrance.

Moscow:

B2

This rock and pop club is a branch of the Moscow club Bunker. Its five floors of entertainment make it the biggest club in Moscow. Dancing and live concerts.
Sadovaya Bolshaya 8. Tel: 495 209 9918. www.b2club.ru. Open: daily noon–6am. Admission charge. Metro: Mayakovskaya.

B B King

Food, live jazz/blues music; visitors may join in playing instruments.
Sadovaya-Samotetchnaya 4/2. Tel: 495

It isn't hard to find a casino in Moscow

699 8206. www.blues.ru. Open: daily noon–midnight. No admission charge except Sat. Metro: Tsvetnoi Bulvar.

Bunker

Drinking, eating, dancing and live music nightly.
Tverskaya Ulitsa 12. Tel: 495 200 1506. Open: non-stop. Admission charge. Metro: Pushkinskaya.

Karma-Bar

Lively and fairly relaxed bar and dance floor with varied programme of parties, DJs, R&B, soul, etc.
Pushechnaya 3. Tel: 495 624 5633. www.karma-bar.ru. Metro: Lubyanka/ Kuznetskiy Most.

Kino (Cinema)

Club restaurant, frequented by personalities from the film industry. Call ahead to reserve a table.
Olimpiyskiy Prospekt 16. Tel: 495 937 7871. www.kino-club.ru. Open: Mon–Wed, Fri noon–2am, Sat 5pm–2am. No admission charge. Metro: Prospekt Mira.

Le Club

Jazz club, live music.
Verkhnaya Radishchevskaya 21. Tel: 495 915 1042. Open: daily noon–midnight. Admission charge. Metro: Taganskaya.

Metelitsa

Dancing, casino, restaurant.
Novy Arbat 21. Tel: 495 691 1130. www.metelitsa.ru. Open: Mon–Thur 9pm–5am, Fri–Sat 9pm–6am. Admission charge. Metro: Arbatskaya.

The Most

Moscow's most exclusive nightspot, frequented by footballers, oligarchs and big-time mafiosi accompanied by their trophy wives.

Ulitsa Kuznetskiy Most.

Tel: 495 660 0706. www.themost.ru.

Metro: Kuznetskiy Most.

Music Town

Jazz, blues and rock music concerts.

Dmitrovka 11. Tel: 495 937 5419.

www.musictownclub.ru.

Metro: Okhotny Ryad.

Night Flight

One of Moscow's best nightclubs with a pricey restaurant and bar. Popular among expats.

Tverskaya Ulitsa 17. Tel: 495 629 4165.

www.nightflight.ru. Open: daily 6pm–5am. Metro: Pushkinskaya.

Petrovich

Restaurant, dancing, concerts.

Myasnitskaya 24. Tel: 495 623 0082.

Open: daily noon–6am. Admission charge. Metro: Chistye Prudy.

Propaganda

Gay-friendly venue.

Bolshoi Zlatoustinskiy Pereulok 7.

Tel: 495 624 5732. www.propaganda moscow.com. Open: daily noon–6am.

Metro: Kitay-Gorod.

R&B Café

Live music, dancing, concerts.

Starovagankovskiy Pereulok 19.

Tel: 495 203 6008. Open: daily noon–midnight. Admission charge.

Metro: Biblioteka imeni Lenina.

St Petersburg:

Café Club Che

Live music nightly with a sophisticated Cuban beat.

Poltavskaya 3. Tel: 277 7600.

www.cafeclubche.ru. Metro: Ploshchad Aleksandra Nevskovo/ Ploshchad Vosstaniya.

Griboedov Club

Open every night, this club offers a wide range of live music.

Voronezhskaya 2a. Tel: 764 4355.

www.griboedovclub.ru.

Metro: Ligovskiy Prospekt.

Fish Fabrique

Live bands from 10pm every night at this St Petersburg institution.

Ligovskiy Prospekt 53.

Tel: 164 4857.

www.fishfabrique.spb.ru.

Metro: Ploshchad Vosstaniya.

Hollywood Nites

Nightclub and casino.

Nevskiy Prospekt 46.

Tel: 311 6077. Metro: Nevskiy Prospekt/Gostiny Dvor.

Premier Casino

Casino and restaurant in historic building.

Nevskiy Prospekt 47. Tel: 703 5370.

www.clubpremier.ru.

Metro: Mayakovskaya.

Red Club

A warehouse venue with live gigs.

Poltavskaya 7. Tel: 717 0000.

www.night.clubred.ru.

Metro: Ploshchad Vosstaniya.

Red Fox Jazz Club

Refreshingly relaxed and informal, this café specialises in live trad-jazz.

Mayakovskovo 50. Tel: 275 4214.

www.rfjc.ru.

Metro: Chernyshevskaya.

Music and theatre

You can find a world-class orchestra or ballet troupe performing on practically any day of the season in Moscow or St Petersburg (most concert halls are closed throughout July and August), and many venues host folk dance and music from every corner of Russia.

CLASSICAL MUSIC
Moscow concert venues:
Dvorets Syezdov (State Kremlin Palace)
Kreml. Tel: 495 917 2336. Metro: Aleksandrovskiy Sad/Borovitskaya.
Moscow Conservatory
Bolshaya Nikitskaya Ulitsa 13. Tel: 495 629 9401. www.mosconsv.ru. Metro: Okhotny Ryad.
Rossiya Concert Hall
Moskvoretskaya Naberezhnaya 1. Tel: 495 298 4350. www.rossia-hall.ru. Metro: Ploshchad Revolyutsii.
Tchaikovsky Concert Hall
Home of the State Symphony Orchestra.
4/31 Triumfalnaya Ploshchad. Tel: 495 699 0658. www.classicalmusic.ru. Metro: Mayakovskaya.

St Petersburg concert venues:
Akademicheskaya Kapella (Academic Capella)
Choral music and small ensembles.
Reki Moyki Naberezhnaya 20. Tel: 314 3649. Metro: Nevskiy Prospekt.

Beloselskiy-Belozerskiy Palace
Home of the St Petersburg City Concert Orchestra.
Nevskiy Prospekt 41. Tel: 311 1384. (Box office noon–6pm.) Metro: Gostiny Dvor.
Filarmoniya (St Petersburg Philharmonia)
Mikhailovskaya Ulitsa 2 (big hall), Nevskiy Prospekt 30 (smaller Glinka hall). Tel: 710 4257. www.philharmonia.spb.ru. Metro: Nevskiy Prospekt.
Oktyabrskiy Concert Hall
Ligovskiy Prospekt 6. Tel: 275 1273. www.bkz.sp.ru. Metro: Ploshchad Vosstaniya.

OPERA AND BALLET
Moscow:
Bolshoi Theatre
Almost 1,000 individuals make up the combined opera and ballet companies of the Bolshoi, but with dwindling state subsidies forcing ever more tours you will be lucky to catch them.
Teatralnaya Ploshchad 1. Tel: 495 250

7317. *www.bolshoi.ru. Metro:*
Teatralnaya Ploshchad. Main theatre is
set to reopen in 2010 after lengthy
repairs. Performances take place on the
New Stage (see p153).
Dvorets Syezdov (State Kremlin Palace)
Home to the State Classical Ballet
Theatre. (*See* Classical Music *for details.*)

St Petersburg:
Ermitazhniy Teatr (Hermitage Theatre)
Dvortsovaya Naberezhnaya 32.
Tel: 579 0226. www.rus-ballet.com.
Metro: Nevskiy Prospekt.
Mariinskiy Theatre
Also known as the Kirov.
Teatralnaya Ploshchad 1. Tel: 326 4141.
www.mariinsky.ru. Metro: Sadovaya.
Mussorgsky Opera and Ballet Theatre
Ploshchad Iskusstv 1. Tel: 595 4305.
Metro: Nevskiy Prospekt.

POP, ROCK AND JAZZ
Moscow (*see also pp148–9*):
Arbat Blues Club
Aksakov Pereulok 11. Tel: 495 291 1546.
Metro: Arbatskaya.
Bunker
Tverskaya Ulitsa 12. Tel: 495 200 1506.
Metro: Tverskaya.
Tabula Rasa
Berezhkovskaya Naberezhnaya 38.
Tel: 499 248 6688. Metro: Kievskaya.

St Petersburg (*see also p149*):
Dzhaz Filarmonik Kholl
(Jazz Philharmonic Hall)
Zagorodniy Prospekt 27. Tel: 764 8565.
Metro: Vladimirskaya.

Griboedov
Voronezhskaya Ulitsa 2a. Tel: 764 4355.
Metro: Ligovskiy Prospekt.
JFC Jazz Club
Shpalernaya Ulitsa 33. Tel: 272 9850.
www.jfc.sp.ru.
Metro: Chernyshevskaya.
Metro
Ligovskiy Prospekt 174. Tel: 766 0211.
www.metroclub.ru.
Metro: Ligovskiy Prospekt.

THEATRE
Moscow:
Chekhov Moscow Art Theatre
Arbat 35. Tel: 495 691 5610.
www.chekhov.ru.
Metro: Smolenskaya.
Lenkom Theatre
Malaya Dmitrovka 6. Tel: 495 699 9668.
www.lenkom.ru. Metro:
Pushkinskaya/Chekhovskaya.
Maliy Theatre
Teatralnaya Ploshchad 1/6.
Tel: 495 624 4083. www.maly.ru.
Metro: Teatralnaya Ploshchad.

St Petersburg:
Aleksandriinskiy Theatre
Ploshchad Ostrovskovo 2. Tel: 380 8050.
http://en.alexandrinsky.ru. Metro:
Nevskiy Prospekt/Gostiny Dvor.
Bolshoi Drama Theatre (BDT)
Reki Fontanki Naberezhnaya 65.
Tel: 310 9242/0401.
Metro: Sennaya Ploshchad.
Maliy Drama Theatre
Ulitsa Rubinshteyna 18. Tel: 713 2078.
Metro: Vladimirskaya.

The Bolshoi

The origins of Moscow's greatest ballet and opera company, the Bolshoi, date back to 1776 when the Moscow procurator, Prince Urusov, formed the first permanent Russian theatre company from the serfs on his estate. They performed in the mansion of his friend Count Vorontsov before the company was established, four years later, as the Petrovskiy Theatre on the site at the end of Ulitsa Petrovka where it remains today.

The monumental classical building that dominates Teatralnaya Ploshchad is the third Bolshoi Theatre. The first burnt down in 1805, as did its successor in 1853. The final version outdoes London's Covent Garden and Milan's La Scala in sheer scale, and is celebrated for its superb acoustics; as the architect remarked: 'It is built like a musical instrument.'

Many great Russian works, most famously Tchaikovsky's ballet Swan Lake, were premiered at the Bolshoi, but it was not until Soviet times, with Moscow again the capital, that it emerged from the shadow of St Petersburg's Mariinskiy Theatre, better known as the Kirov. During the Bolshoi's modern heyday in the 1960s and 1970s, opera houses around the world were packed with audiences mesmerised by the company's performances of Stravinsky's Petrushka and Khachaturian's Gayane with its breathtaking 'Sabre Dance'.

Those days are over. The Bolshoi's repertoire has been cut along with once lavish state subsidies, and top dancers are loaned abroad to raise much-needed funds. Each season is punctuated by pay disputes and strikes by the company's 900 members. A long-standing feud was brought to a head in 1995 when the much-loved artistic director resigned after a battle with theatre authorities; the dancers promptly walked out of a performance in protest. When they appeared in court a few days later, the capital was left to wonder how long the flagship of Russia's 200-year-old ballet tradition would survive into the 21st century.

The Bolshoi is currently going through its 234th season, employing more than 2,500 people. Many world-famous opera singers have performed on its stage – Montserrat Caballé, Luciano Pavarotti, José Carreras and many others. It also regularly holds performances by theatres from Germany, Sweden, the USA and many other countries. While the Bolshoi is closed for repairs (set to run until at least 2013), performances will take place on the New Stage next door. *www.bolshoi.ru*

The Bolshoi in all its glory

Festivals

Today new holidays marking turning points in the struggle against Soviet power take their place alongside resurrected religious festivals in the Orthodox calendar. Landmarks in Bolshevik history that were once solemnly celebrated are now simply excuses for a bit of partying. Both Moscow and St Petersburg host a series of annual arts and music festivals.

December/January

December/January: The **Arts Square Winter Festival** is a music festival which is held by the Philharmonia, with a different theme taking centre stage every year.

25 December–5 January: **Russian Winter festival**. A secular celebration with family parties and cultural programmes at the two cities' main venues (*see pp150–51*). **New Year's Day** (1 January) is Russia's foremost holiday, with present-giving by Ded-Moroz, 'Grandfather Frost' (*see p136*).

7 January: **Orthodox Christmas**, with all-night liturgies in church.

13/14 January: **Orthodox New Year** – not officially a holiday but treated as such.

27 January: **Breaking of the Siege of Leningrad**. A public holiday in St Petersburg.

February/March

23 February: **Defenders of the Motherland Day**. The successor of Red Army Day, no longer a national holiday, but still an occasion of drinking parties.

February/March: **Maslenitsa**, marking the end of winter and the beginning of Lent. Not a public holiday but celebrated by huge feasting (*see p136*).

8 March: **International Women's Day**. A day off for everybody except city flower-sellers.

March/April

Easter, *paskha*, is the chief Orthodox festival. Children colour eggs and enjoy the traditional dish of sweetened curds with raisins, also called *paskha*. *www.easterfestival.ru*

April/May

End of April/early May: **Musical Spring** festival in St Petersburg. International concerts at main venues (*see pp150–51*).

May/June

1/2 May: **International Working People's Solidarity Day**. A day for demonstrations by communists and a holiday for everyone else.

9 May: **Victory Day**. Celebrates the end of World War II in Europe. Parades and wreath-laying in Moscow's Park Pobedy and at the Tomb of the Unknown Soldier, and processions of veterans along Nevskiy Prospekt in St Petersburg.

12 June: **Russian Independence Day**. Commemorates Russia's secession from the Soviet Union in 1991.

Annually in June: **Moscow Film Festival** (*www.moscowfilmfestival.ru*, see English-language press for details).

June/July

21 June–1 July: **White Nights Festival** in St Petersburg. Long nights celebrating the summer solstice when the sun virtually never sets. Informal partying on the streets, plus concerts on Yelagin Island (*Chernaya Rechka metro, then overland transport heading down Primorskoe Prospekt to the bridge*). Crowds gather on the river embankment to watch the bridges being raised just after 1.30am.

August/October

First four days of August: **Love Street Festival** in Moscow. Off-beat street entertainments and fringe art around Pokrovskiy Bulvar (*metro: Chistye Prudy*) and in Moscow's clubs (*see pp148–9*).

6 September (or nearest Sat): **Moscow City Day**. Parade and festivities.

8 September: **Siege of Leningrad Day**. Not a public holiday, but a day of mourning and remembrance in St Petersburg.

Late Sept/early Oct (Moscow): **Solomon Mikoels International Festival**. Drama, music, film and literature.

November

7 November (25 October by old Russian calendar): **Revolution Day**. Once celebrated by the Soviet arsenal rolling across Red Square and now marked (unofficially) by communist marches.

Mid-November: **Autumn Rhythms** jazz festival in St Petersburg, centred on the city's jazz clubs (*see p151*).

Russian dancers in traditional costumes

Children

Snowstorms and sledging make the Russian winter fun for children of all ages, but even in the summer months Moscow and St Petersburg have plenty to keep youngsters interested.

MUSEUMS

Those in Moscow likely to appeal to youngsters include the Polytechnic, Space Travel, Armed Forces museums and the Borodino Battle Panorama (*see pp65, 79, 84, 85*).

Life-size effigies of Russia's good, bad and ugly in Moscow's **Waxworks Museum** appeal to children of all ages.
Tverskaya Ulitsa 14. Open: Tue 11am–7pm, Wed–Sun 11am–6pm. Metro: Pushkinskaya.

In St Petersburg, Peter the Great's extraordinary Kunstkamera (Museum of Anthropology and Ethnography – *see p122*) will capture any teenager's imagination. The Historical Waxworks in the Stroganov Palace, the Ethnographic and Naval museums (*see pp109, 120, 129*), as well as the Cruiser *Aurora* (*see pp121–2*), may also prove popular.

PARKS

Russian amusement parks have a long way to go if they want to rival Euro-Disney, but what they lack in high-tech rides is made up for by the holiday atmosphere and low fares.

Park imeni A M Gorkovo (Gorky Park) in Moscow has a roller coaster, boating lake and magnificent Ferris wheel.
Krymskiy Val Ulitsa 9. Tel: 495 637 0707. Metro: Park Kultury/Oktyabrskaya.
Central Park of Culture and Rest in St Petersburg boasts a small animal enclosure and is a venue for fun events on national holidays and festivals.
Elagin Ostrov 4. Metro: Krestovskiy Ostrov.

RIVER RIDES

A cruise in a motor launch among the canals of St Petersburg restores the culture-sated, young or old (*see pp138–9*). Hydrofoil and pleasure boat trips tour the Moskva River in warmer months. You can board at several locations, but the most convenient are next to Kievsky Vokzal (Kiev railway station) and on the embankment at Gorky Park.

THEATRE AND CIRCUS

Puppet shows are a well-loved Russian tradition, and though they are in Russian, small children will be fascinated.

Moscow:

Obraztsov Puppet Theatre
Sadovaya-Samotyochnaya Ulitsa 3. Tel: 495 699 3310. www.puppet.ru. Metro: Mayakovskaya.

St Petersburg:

Bryantsev Theatre for Young Viewers
Pionerskaya Ploshchad 1. Tel: 164 1124. Metro: Pushkinskaya.

Demmeni Puppet Theatre
Nevskiy Prospekt 52. Tel: 571 2156. Metro: Moskovskiye Vorota.

No trip to Russia is complete without a visit to the circus. The shows are spectacular, with animals, Cossack acrobats and the world's best clowns.

Moscow:

State Circus (Tsirk Nikulina)
Much improved with acts from all over the world; thoroughly entertaining. *Tsvetnoi Bulvar 13. Tel: 495 625 8970. www.circusnikulin.ru. Metro: Tsvetnoi Bulvar.*

St Petersburg:

Circus on Fontanka
Reki Fontanki Naberezhnaya 3. Tel: 570 5390. Metro: Gostiny Dvor.

VIEWS OF THE CITY

Some of the best views of Moscow are from Sparrow Hills (*Metro: Universitet/ Vorobyovy Gory*) where there is woodland for the children to run around in. The rooftop panoramas from St Isaac's Cathedral in St Petersburg are breathtaking (*see pp115–16*).

ZOOS

Moscow and St Petersburg zoos must rank as two of the least attractive in the world. Nevertheless, most children are likely to spend a happy afternoon there.

Moskovskiy Zoopark (Moscow Zoo)
Bolshaya Gruzinskaya Ulitsa 1. Tel: 499 255 6034. www.moscowzoo.ru. Open: Tue–Sun summer 10am–8pm; winter 10am–5pm. Admission charge. Metro: Barrikadnaya/ Krasnopresnenskaya.

Zoopark ('Leningrad' Zoo)
Aleksandrovskiy Park 1. Tel: 232 8250. www.spbzoo.ru. Open: 10am–9pm. Admission charge. Metro: Gorkovskaya.

There's plenty to keep children entertained at Gorky Park

Sport

As one of the world's greatest sporting nations, Russia has a lot to offer sports fans of almost every persuasion. You can enjoy first-rate football and ice hockey matches for a fraction of the cost at home, and there is ample opportunity to get involved yourself – from skiing and skating to hunting wild boar or flying a Soviet jet! And at the end of the day, you can treat yourself to a traditional Russian steam bath.

BATHHOUSES

Getting steamed up at the *banya* is not so much a way of getting clean as a whole Russian subculture in itself. Cognoscenti of the *banya* do not expect to spend less than three hours relaxing in the hot and cold rooms, playing pool, working out, philosophising and drinking beer – all, of course, completely nude.

Remember to take your own towel, toiletries and sandals. Birch twig *veniki*, for mutual exfoliation, are sold on the premises. Sexes strictly segregated.

Moscow:
Sandunovskiye Banyi
The best *banya* by far, their elegant décor making them a sight in themselves.
Neglinnaya Ulitsa 14.
Tel: 495 628 4633. www.sanduny.ru.
Metro: Chekhovskaya.

St Petersburg:
Yamskiye Banyi
Dostoevskovo 9. Tel: 312 5836.
Open: Wed–May. Metro: Vladimirskaya.

BOWLING ALLEYS
Moscow:
Aurora
Profsoyuznaya 154. Tel: 495 339 4187.
Open: daily 11am–5am.
Metro: Tyopliy Stan.
Bi-Ba-Bo
Karmanitskiy Pereulok 9. Tel: 495 937 4337. Open: daily 3pm–5am.
Metro: Smolenskaya.
Champion
The largest, with 20 lanes, pool and snooker, big-screen TV, cafés and bars.
Leningradskoe Shosse 16. Tel: 495 747 5000. www.champion.ru.
Open: daily.
Metro: Voykovskaya.

St Petersburg:
Aquatoria *Vyborgskaya*
Naberezhnaya 61. Tel: 245 2030.
Metro: Vyborgskaya.
Lightning Ball
Korablestroiteley Ulitsa 14 (Pribaltiyskaya Hotel). Tel: 329 2489.
Metro: Primorskaya.

CROSS-COUNTRY SKIING

Flat terrain rules out downhill skiing, but the cross-country variety is hugely popular. Head for any of the outlying parks in winter. Skis can be acquired at most sports shops for a modest outlay (*see p143*).

FOOTBALL

Russians adore football, but hooliganism and racism are common in stadiums. Tickets are sold on the day at stadiums. The season is from March to October.

Moscow:

Moscow's main football teams, Torpedo, Dinamo and CSKA, play respectively at: **Sportivnaya Arena Luzhniki** (Luzhniki Stadium) *Luzhnetskaya Naberezhnaya 24. Tel: 495 785 9717. Metro: Vorobyovy Gory.* **Stadion Dinamo** (Dinamo Stadium) *Leningradskiy Prospekt 36. Tel: 495 612 7172. www.fcdinamo.ru. Metro: Dinamo.*

Outdoor skating in Kirov Central Park, St Petersburg

Stadion CSKA
Leningradskiy Prospekt 39. Tel: 495 612 0780. Metro: Aeroport/Dinamo.

St Petersburg:

Zenit FC plays at **Petrovskiy Stadium** (Kirov Stadium) on Petrovskiy Island. *Morskoi Prospekt 1. Tel: 328 8901. www.fc-zenit.ru. Metro: Sportivnaya.*

GOLF

Popular with Moscow's *nouveaux riches*, the **Moscow City Golf Club** also accepts green fees.
*Ulitsa Dovzhenko 1.
Tel: 495 921 2855. www.mcgc.ru.
Metro: Universitet, then bus 67 to Mosfilmovskaya Ulitsa.*

HORSE RACING

Fast-action buggy racing in the centre of Moscow on Wednesdays and weekends at the **Hippodrome**.
Begovaya Ulitsa 22. Tel: 495 945 5059. Metro: Belorusskaya.

HORSE RIDING

It is hard to beat the romance of riding through birch forests in springtime or taking a horse-drawn sleigh ride after a fresh snowfall.

Moscow:

Yauza Stables

Offers lessons and riding in pleasant woodland 8km (5 miles) northeast of the city centre.
*Ulitsa Bogatyrskiy Most 17.
Tel: 499 268 2868.*

HUNTING

The 55,000-ha (135,900-acre) **Ozerinskoe Reserve** outside Moscow was former Soviet leader Leonid Brezhnev's favourite hunting ground. A well-kept lodge includes a restaurant that will roast the results of the day's sport in the evening.
www.russianhunting.com

ICE HOCKEY

When it is too cold for football, passions switch to ice hockey, played at world standard in Russia's two big cities. International matches are advertised in the local press. Tickets at stadiums.

Moscow:

Moscow's football teams also have hockey squads. CSKA play at the CSKA Arena, Torpedo at the Luzhniki Stadium.

CSKA Arena: *Leningradskiy Prospekt 39a. Tel: 495 225 2600. Metro: Aeroport/Dinamo.*

Luzhniki Stadium: *Luzhnetskaya Naberezhnaya 24. Tel: 495 785 9717. Metro: Vorobyovy Gory.*

St Petersburg:

Ledoviy Dvorets (Ice Palace)
Pyatiletok Prospekt 1. Tel: 718 6620. www.newarena.spb.ru. Metro: Prospekt Bolshevikov.

ICE SKATING

You can skate the icy boulevards of Moscow's Gorky Park in winter or visit one of many covered rinks. Some places hire out skates, but bring extra pairs of socks in case your size is not available.

Moscow:

Evropeysky
Ploshchad Kievskovo Voksala 2. Tel: 495 921 4444. www.euro-katok.ru. Open: hours vary according to the season. Metro: Kievskaya.

Gorky Park
The rink turns into a disco on ice in the evenings. Skate hire available.
Krymskiy Val Ulitsa 9. Metro: Park Kultury.

Sokolniki Palace of Sports
Three indoor rinks.
Sokolnicheskiy Val 1b. Tel: 495 645 2065. Metro: Sokolniki (line 1).

St Petersburg:

Palace Square
Some 5,000 square metres of ice in front of the Hermitage make this Europe's largest skating rink.
Dvortsovaya Ploshchad. Open: winter only. Metro: Nevskiy Prospekt.

JOGGING

Moscow's expats gather at 3pm outside the Tchaikovsky Concert Hall on Sundays all year round for the Hash House Harriers' run. Lighthearted fun.
www.moscowharriers.itgo.com. Metro: Mayakovskaya.

SAILING

Call ahead to confirm availability.

Moscow:

Spartak Yacht Club charters yachts and instructors on an hourly rate and can

arrange longer trips to St Petersburg or Astrakhan on the Volga delta.
Dolgoprudniy Town, Naberezhnaya Ulitsa 4a. Tel: 495 408 2500. www.spartak.ws. 5km (3 miles) along Dmitrovskoe Shosse or by elektrichka from Savyolovskiy Vokzal.

St Petersburg:
Neva Yacht Club organises sailing in the Gulf of Finland and can also supply motorboats.
Naberezhnaya Martynova 94, Krestovskiy Island. Tel: 235 2722. www.clubneva.ru. Metro: Krestovskiy Ostrov.

SWIMMING
Moscow:
Chayka
Turchaninov Pereulok 1/3. Tel: 499 246 1344. Open: Mon–Sat 7am–10pm, Sun 8.30am–8pm. Metro: Park Kultury.
Luzhniki Olympic Swimming Pool
Luzhnetskaya Naberezhnaya 24. Tel: 495 637 0764. Open: daily 8am–8pm. Metro: Vorobyovy Gory.

St Petersburg:
Dinamo Sports Centre
A gym which also has an indoor pool for the colder months.
Prospekt Dinamo 44. Tel: 235 4717. Metro: Krestovskiy Ostrov. Pool closed: Jun–Sept.

TENNIS
The country's best compete against foreign stars in Moscow's Kremlin Cup. See local press for details. You can play at the following venues.

Moscow:
Dinamo Centr
Ulitsa Petrovka 26. Tel: 495 209 6809. Open: daily, outdoor 7am–9pm, indoor 11am–11pm. Metro: Okhotny Ryad/Teatralnaya.
CSKA Tennis Palace
Leningradskiy Prospekt 39a. Tel: 495 213 6547. Open: daily 7am–midnight. Metro: Aeroport/Dinamo.

St Petersburg:
Lightning
Primorskoe Prospekt 50. Tel: 430 6884. Open: daily 8am–10pm. Metro: Staraya Derevnya.

WORKOUT
Both Moscow and St Petersburg have good selections of well-equipped gyms.
Moscow:
Chaika Sport Complex
Turchaninov Pereulok 1/3. Tel: 499 246 1344. Metro: Park Kultury.
City Fitness
4 Dobryninskiy Pereulok 8/10. Tel: 495 775 8587. www.cityfit.ru. Metro: Dobryninskaya.

St Petersburg:
Neptune Hotel
Gym, swimming pool, sauna, solarium, Turkish bath, aerobics classes.
Obvodnovo Kanala Naberezhnaya 93a. Tel: 324 4696/4610. Metro: Pushkinskaya.
Planet Fitness
In Grand Hotel Europe, Mikhailovskaya Ulitsa 1/7. Tel: 329 6597.

Food and drink

As Russian tastes continue to develop, Russia is rapidly overcoming its once well-deserved reputation as a gastronomic disaster area. In Moscow and St Petersburg at least, the days of barely edible food and appalling service are all but a distant memory and the hungry traveller can look forward to a top-class introduction to one of the world's most underrated cuisines.

Eating habits

Most Russians are less concerned with *what* they eat than with getting enough of it. Many are struggling to maintain any eating habit at all. Consequently, tourists should bear in mind that they are in a somewhat artificial position. Although Caspian caviar and Siberian salmon are indeed key elements of the

Blini, served with red caviar

traditional menu, most citizens get by on large quantities of bread, potatoes and cabbage.

The Russian breakfast is generally a light affair centred on a good deal of strong, black tea, cold meat and cheese. It is often accompanied by *kefir*, a yoghurt-like drink much praised for its stomach-settling qualities the morning after the night before. Hotel breakfasts may add extra delicacies such as *blini* (pancakes) with honey.

Soups are very much a lunchtime dish, served piping hot and with a generous spoonful of soured cream stirred in. *Pirozhki* (savoury stuffed doughnuts), a variation on ravioli called *pelmyeni* and the southern favourite of *shashlyk* – meat kebabs – are also midday staples, often served up with boiled buckwheat or a mayonnaise-doused salad. A slice of black bread, as with any meal, is always on offer.

Dinner is easily the most elaborate meal and, if eating out, Russians like to make an occasion of it. Hot and cold *zakuski* (hors d'œuvre) – typically smoked fish, wild mushrooms, hams and *blini* with red or black caviar – are almost enough in themselves, but Russians spread the load with dancing, philosophical debate and toasting throughout the evening. Traditionally, there is little concept of a quiet night out for two!

Drinking

Deeply ingrained in the culture despite occasional efforts to eradicate it, drinking on a grand scale is a national tradition and is focused firmly on the vodka bottle. Vodka (*see p171*) is drunk neat in shots, preferably chilled, and followed up with a bite of marinaded fish or pickled cucumber. Be warned – Russian tolerance of vodka is famously higher than that of most tourists. One or two toasts are unavoidable, but then exercise a little caution, remembering that vodka-induced drunkenness steals up extremely rapidly.

The other great Russian love is tea. Drunk in copious quantities and without milk, tea is often served with a side saucer of home-made jam in place of sugar. Coffee is also highly prized, often presented Turkish-style and heavily sweetened unless you specify otherwise (*byez sakhara* – without sugar).

Table etiquette

A meal out in Russia involves a greater emphasis on etiquette than in the West, with men expected to seat their partners and administer all drinks. (Single women should never be seated at the table corner – as any *babushka* will tell you, this means they will not marry for seven years!)

It is bad luck to leave empty bottles on the table, bad form not to finish opened ones, and a round of drinks should always be preceded by a toast. Toasts to health (*za vashye zdorovye!*) require you to down your glassful in one. Smoking is acceptable at all junctures of the evening and non-smoking areas in restaurants are rare indeed.

If invited back home to eat, you ought to bring along a contribution to the meal (chocolates or a bottle of something) and flowers for your hostess.

Pirozhki for sale

Menu guide

(stressed syllables in italics)

Meals
ЗАВТРАК – *zah*vtrak – **breakfast**
ОБЕД – ab*yed* – **lunch**
УЖИН – *oo*zhin – **dinner**
ЗАКУСКИ – za*koo*ski – **starters/
appetisers**
САЛАТ – sa*laht* – **salad**
СУП – *soop* – **soup**
ПЕРВЫЕ БЛЮДА – p*yer*viye *blyoo*da –
first course, usually soup
ВТОРЫЕ БЛЮДА – vtor*eeye blyoo*da
– **second or 'hot' course**
ДЕСЕРТ – de*syert* – **dessert**
ФРУКТЫ – *frook*ti – **fruit**

Meat and fish
МЯСО – *myasa* – **meat**
ГОВЯДИНА – gav*yahd*ina – **beef**
СВИНИНА – svin*eena* – **pork**
БАРАНИНА – ba*rahn*ina –
lamb/mutton
ТЕЛЯТИНА – tel*yaht*ina – **veal**
КУРИЦА – *koo*ritsa – **chicken**
КОЛБАСА – kolba*sah* – **sausage**
РЫБА – *ri*ba – **fish**
ЛОСОСЬ/ГОРБУША/СЁМГА –
la*sos*/gar*boo*sha/*syom*ga – **salmon**
ТРЕСКА – tres*ka* – **cod**
ФОРЕЛЬ – far*yel* – **trout**
ОСЕТРИНА/СЕВРЮГА – asye*treen*a/
se*vryoo*ga – **sturgeon**
ЧЁРНАЯ/КРАСНАЯ ИКРА –
*chyor*naya/*kras*naya i*krah* –
black/red caviar

Vegetables, fruit and other foods
МОРКОВЬ – mar*kohv* – **carrots**
СВЁКЛА – *svyok*la – **beetroot**
КАПУСТА – ka*poos*ta – **cabbage**
КАРТОФЕЛЬ – kar*tof*el – **potatoes**
ЛУК – *look* – **onion**
ОГУРЕЦ – agoo*rets* – **cucumber**
ПОМИДОР – pomi*dor* – **tomatoes**

ЯБЛОКО – *yah*bloka – **apple**
АПЕЛЬСИН – apel*seen* – **orange**
ДЫНЯ – *deen*ya – **melon**
БАНАН – ba*nahn* – **banana**
ЯЙЦА – *yait*sa – **eggs**
РИС – *rees* – **rice**
ХЛЕБ – *khlyeb* – **bread**
МОРОЖЕНОЕ – mar*ozh*enoye –
ice cream
ТОРТ – *tort* – **cake, gâteau**

Cooking methods
КОПЧЁНЫЙ – kap*chyony* – **smoked**
ВАРЁНЫЙ – var*yony* – **boiled**
ЖАРЕНЫЙ – *zha*reny – **fried**
ПЕЧЁНЫЙ – pe*chyony* – **baked**
СОЛЁНЫЙ – sal*yony* – **salted**

Traditional dishes
ВИНЕГРЕТ – vinye*gryet* – **diced
vegetable salad**
САЛАТ ОЛИВЬЕ/СТОЛИЧНЫЙ
САЛАТ – sa*laht* oliv*yeh*, stol*eech*ny
sa*laht* – **diced meat, potatoes and
vegetables in mayonnaise or soured
cream**
БОРЩ – *borshch* – **beetroot soup**
ЩИ – *shchi* – **cabbage soup**
УХА – oo*kha* – **fish soup**
СОЛЯНКА – sal*yahn*ka – **thick fish or
meat soup with potatoes**
ОКРОШКА – a*krosh*ka – **cold soup
made from salad, cold meat
and kvas**
ГРИБЫ – gri*bi* – **mushrooms, often
marinaded or baked in soured
cream**
БЛИНЫ – bl*ini* – **small pancakes,
traditionally served with soured
cream and caviar**
ПЕЛЬМЕНИ – pel*myen*i – **a heavy
version of ravioli served in soured
cream**

ПИРОЖКИ – pirozh*ki* – **meat, cabbage, etc. in fried dough**

БЕФСТРОГАНОВ – byef*stroh*ganov – **beef stroganoff, strips of beef in sour cream sauce**

КОТЛЕТЫ ПО КИЕВСКИЙ – kaht*lyeh*ti pa *kee*yevsky – **chicken Kiev**

КУЛЕБЯКА – kooli*byah*ka – **generally fish, especially salmon, en croûte**

ГОЛУБЦЫ – golubt*si* – **cabbage leaves stuffed with meat and rice**

ЖАРКОЕ – *zhar*koye – **spicy meat casserole in earthenware pot**

ШАШЛЫК – shash*lyk* – **kebabed meat**

ХАЧАПУРИ – khacha*poori* – **Caucasian flat bread stuffed with cheese**

Sauces and condiments

СМЕТАНА – sme*tahn*a – **soured cream**

МАЙОНЕЗ – maiyon*ehz* – **mayonnaise**

ТОМАТНЫЙ СОУС – to*maht*ny sohs – **tomato sauce**

СЛИВОЧНОЕ МАСЛО – *slee*vochnoye *mah*sla – **butter**

СОЛЬ – *sohl* – **salt**

ПЕРЕЦ – py*erets* – **pepper**

ГОРЧИЦА – gar*cheet*sa – **mustard**

САХАР – s*akh*ar – **sugar**

Drinks

ВОДА – va*dah* – **water**

МИНЕРАЛЬНАЯ ВОДА (С ГАЗОМ/БЕЗ ГАЗА)– miner*ahl*naya va*dah* (s *gah*zom/byez *gah*za) – **mineral water (carbonated/still)**

СОК – sok – **fruit juice**

БЕЛОЕ/КРАСНОЕ ВИНО – bye*loye*/kras*noye* vi*noh* – **white/red wine**

СЛАДКОЕ/СУХОЕ – slad*koye*/su*khoye* – **sweet/dry**

ВОДКА – *vod*ka – **vodka**

КОНЬЯК – kon*yahk* – **brandy**

ПИВО – *pee*va – **beer**

ШАМПАНСКОЕ – sham*pahn*skoye – **'champagne' (Russian sparkling wine)**

ЛИКЁРЫ – lik*yori* – **liqueurs**

ЧАЙ (С МОЛОКОМ/С ЛИМОНОМ/С САХАРОМ/БЕЗ САХАРА) – chai (s mala*kom*/s li*moh*nom/s *sakh*arom/byez *sakh*ara) – **tea (with milk, lemon, sugar, without sugar)**

КОФЕ (С САХАРОМ/БЕЗ САХАРА) – *koh*fye (s *sakh*arom/byez *sakh*ara) – **coffee (with/without sugar)**

Useful words and phrases

РЕСТОРАН – ryesta*rahn* – **restaurant**

КАФЕ – ka*feh* – **café**

БАР – *bar* – **bar**

МЕНЮ – men*yoo* – **menu**

ОФИЦИАНТ – afits*yant* – **waiter**

СТАКАН – sta*kahn* – **glass (tumbler)**

БОКАЛ – ba*kahl* – **glass (wine glass)**

ЧАШКА – *chash*ka – **cup**

ТАРЕЛКА – tar*yel*ka – **plate**

НОЖ – *nozh* – **knife**

ВИЛКА – *veel*ka – **fork**

ЛОЖКА – *lozh*ka – **spoon**

ТУАЛЕТ – tooah*lyet* – **washroom**

ПЕПЕЛЬНИЦА – *pye*pelneetsa – **ashtray**

МОЖНО ЕЩЁ ... ? – *mozh*na ye*shyoh* ...? – **May I have some more ...?**

ЭТО НЕСЪЕДОБНО – *eh*ta nyesye*dob*na – **This is inedible**

МОЖНО СЧЁТ, ПОЖАЛУЙСТА? – *mozh*na shyot, pa*zhal*sta? – **May I have the bill, please?**

СДАЧИ НЕ НАДО – *sdach*i nye *na*da – **Keep the change**

НА ЧАЙ – na *chai* – **tip**

RESTAURANTS, BARS AND CAFÉS

The choice of good eating and drinking establishments in both cities is rapidly expanding, though quality and price level seesaw dramatically. These listings concentrate on the tried and trusted.

An increasing number of restaurants accept credit cards, but it is wise to come well supplied with roubles. Very few now take foreign currency in cash.

Vegetarians are poorly catered for in general. (If necessary, ask the waiter for help: *Ya nye yem myaso* – I don't eat meat; *Kakiye oo vas blyooda byez myasa?* – What do you have without meat?)

Always book in advance (ask your hotel to do this).

Tip as you would in Europe (but only if you are happy with the level of service provided). The cloakroom attendant will also expect a small gratuity.

Price guide

Poorer Russians seldom eat out, so many restaurants are in the medium-to-expensive bracket. As a rough guide, reckon on the following categories per head without alcohol:

- ★ less than 500R
- ★★ 500R–750R
- ★★★ 750R–1,500R
- ★★★★ more than 1,500R

Beer costs between 100R and 250R per 500ml; vodka costs 100R to 220R per domestic bottle, twice that for imported. Wine and champagne vary considerably, locally produced brands being greatly cheaper.

MOSCOW
RESTAURANTS

Felicita ★

Grab a quick pizza or pasta dish at this conveniently located mock-Italian eatery just off Tverskaya Ulitsa.
Sadovaya Bolshaya 3. Tel: 495 650 3401. Open: noon–midnight. Metro: Mayakovskaya.

Pirogi na Nikolskoy ★

Inexpensive dishes and laid-back coffees by day; cocktails after dark.
Nikolskaya Ulitsa 19/21. Tel: 495 921 5827. Open: 24 hours. Metro: Lubyanka.

Da Cicco ★/★★

This *trattoria* is great for pizza and pasta.
Profsoyuznaya 13/12. Tel: 495 125 1196. www.cicco.ru. Open: noon–11pm. Metro: Profsoyuznaya.

Barrandov ★★

New Czech-style beer hall and restaurant named after Prague's famous film studios. Reasonably priced food and a lively atmosphere.
Preobrazhenskaya Ploshchad 6. Tel: 495 247 1608. Open: noon–midnight. Metro: Preobrazhenskaya Ploshchad.

Kvass ★★

Traditional Russian cooking in nostalgic surroundings.
Ulitsa Sadovaya-Chernogryazskaya 20. Tel: 495 917 5669. Open: noon–midnight. Metro: Krasnye Vorota.

The Real Mccoy ★★

Pop into this 'speakeasy' in one of the Stalin skyscrapers to enjoy a snack, steak or cocktail.
Kudrinskaya Ploshchad. Tel: 499 255

4144. www.mccoy.ru.
Open: 24 hours. Metro:
Barrikadnaya.

Botanika ★★/★★★
Central and stylish, with
tasty and affordable food.
Bolshaya Gruzinskaya 61.
Tel: 495 254 0064. Open:
11am–10pm. Metro:
Belorusskaya.

Noev Kovcheg ★★/★★★
Fine Armenian food.
Maliy Ivanovskiy Pereulok
9. Tel: 495 917 0717.
www.noevkovcheg.ru.
Open: noon–midnight.
Metro: Kitay-Gorod.

Pushkin ★★/★★★
Prize-winning café and
restaurant, Russian food.
Tverskoi Bulvar 26a.
Tel: 495 629 5590. Open:
noon–midnight. Metro:
Pushkinskaya.

Remi ★★/★★★
If you fancy going all
Gallic in the Russian
capital, do it here.
Bolshoi Patriarshy
Pereulok 12. Tel: 495 691
7655. www.remycafe.ru.
Open: 11am–11pm.
Metro: Mayakovskaya.

**1 Krasnaya
Ploshchad ★★★**
Located in the Historical
Museum, this restaurant
serves up tasty Imperial-
era cuisine.

Krasnaya Ploshchad 1.
Tel: 495 692 1196.
www.redsquare.ru.
Open: noon–midnight.
Metro: Ploshchad
Revolyutsii/Okhotny
Ryad.

Baan Thai ★★★
Authentic and reliable
Thai favourites.
Dorogomilovskaya
Bolshaya 11.
Tel: 499 240 0597.
www.baanthai.ru.
Open: noon–midnight.
Metro: Kievskaya.

Damas ★★★
Cutting-edge eatery with
a superb blend of oriental
and European dishes.
Maroseyka 8.
Tel: 495 628 8080.
www.damas-rest.ru.
Open: noon till late.
Metro: Kitay-Gorod.

Shinok ★★★
Ukrainian restaurant
offering typical dishes.
Ulitsa 1905 Goda 2.
Tel: 495 651 8101.
www.shinok.ru.
Open: 24 hours.
Metro: 1905 Goda Ulitsa.

Tiflis ★★★
A popular Georgian
restaurant with an
upmarket flavour. All
ingredients are sourced
in Georgia.

Ulitsa Ostozhenka 32.
Tel: 499 766 9728. Open:
noon–midnight. Metro:
Park Kultury.

Carre Blanc ★★★★
French haute cuisine.
Seleznevskaya 19/2. Tel:
495 258 4403.
www.carreblanc.ru. Open:
noon–midnight. Metro:
Novoslobodskaya.

Godunov ★★★★
Located in the former
Zaikonospassky
Monastery, this opulent
establishment has a
traditional menu and
nightly folk shows.
Teatralnaya Ploshchad 5.
Tel: 495 698 4490.
www.godunov.net.
Open: noon–midnight.
Metro: Teatralnaya.

Uzbekistan ★★★★
Uzbek, Arabic and
Chinese cuisine.
Neglinnaya 29/14.
Tel: 495 623 0585. www.
uzbek-rest.ru. Open:
noon–midnight.
Metro: Teatralnaya.

**ST PETERSBURG
RESTAURANTS**
Khachapurnaya ★
Delightful and
inexpensive Georgian
eatery with a central
location.

Ligovskiy Prospekt 154.
Tel: 766 5829. Open:
10am–11pm. Metro:
Ploshchad Vosstaniya.

NEP ★
1920s-style cabaret and restaurant.
Reki Moyki Naberezhnaya
37. Tel: 312 3722. Open:
Mon–Tue noon–11pm,
Wed–Sat noon–1am.
Metro: Nevskiy Prospekt.

Sakartvelo ★
St Petersburg's most authentic Georgian restaurant.
12-ya Liniya 13.
Tel: 947 7878. Open:
noon–11pm. Metro:
Mayakovskaya.

Dyushez ★/★★
Located on the Vyborg Side, this popular Caucasian eatery is light on the wallet.

Reservations are recommended.
Pirogovskaya
Naberezhnaya 17/1.
Tel: 320 4929.
Open: 24 hours.
Metro: Finlyandskiy
Vokzal.

Chekhov ★★
Travel back in time to Chekhov's era at this elegant restaurant north of the Peter and Paul Fortress.
Ulitsa Petropavlovskaya 4.
Tel: 234 4511.
Open: noon–11pm.
Metro: Petrogradskaya.

Kalinka-Malinka ★★
The best of national cuisine. Great variety of folk entertainment.
Italianskaya Ulitsa 5.
Tel: 314 2681.
www.kalinka-malinka.

spb.ru. Metro: Nevskiy
Prospekt.

Pirosmani ★★
Cosy Georgian restaurant with old Tbilisi interiors.
Bolshoi Prospekt 14.
Tel: 235 6456. Metro:
Sportivnaya.

Tandoori Nights ★★
St Petersburg's most luxurious Indian restaurant equipped with a real clay tandoori oven.
Voznesenskiy Prospekt 4.
Tel: 312 8772. Open:
11am–midnight. Metro:
Sadovaya.

U Schweika ★★
Feast on Bohemian belly-fillers at this Czech-themed restaurant. Live music and Czech beer.
Kirochnaya Ulitsa 8.
Tel: 273 4196. Open:

Russia offers a range of stylish restaurants in romantic settings, but at a price

Thur–Sat noon–2am,
Sun–Wed noon–1am.
Metro: Chernyshevskaya.

Literaturnoe
Café ★★/★★★
Pushkin's favourite.
Nevskiy Prospekt 18.
Tel: 312 6057. Metro:
Nevskiy Prospekt.

Da Vinci ★★★
Five different cuisines in
this restaurant-bar with
live music.
Malaya Morskaya Ulitsa
15. Tel: 571 0173.
www.davinci.spb.ru.
Open: noon–2am.
Metro: Nevskiy Prospekt.

Idiot ★★★
One of the best vegetarian
restaurants in the city.
Reki Moyki Naberezhnaya
82. Tel: 315 1675.
Metro: Sadovaya.

Kavkaz Bar ★★★
Live music, more than 70
excellent Georgian wines.
Karavannaya Ulitsa 18.
Tel: 312 1665.
www.kavkazbar.ru.
Open: (café) 11am–8pm,
(restaurant) 11am–1am.
Metro: Gostiny
Dvor/Nevskiy Prospekt.

New Island ★★★
European cuisine. Ship
restaurant that is
occasionally visited by
the president.

Rumyantsevskiy Spusk.
Tel: 320 2120. Open:
11am–11pm. Metro:
Vasileostrovskaya.

1913 ★★★/★★★★
A traditional Russian
restaurant serving classic
but uncomplicated fare.
Voznesenskiy Prospekt
13/2. Tel: 315 5148.
Open: noon–1am.
Metro: Nevskiy
Prospekt/Sadovaya.

Landskrona ★★★★
Petersburg's best. Fine
dining and rooftop
patio.
Nevskiy Palace Hotel,
Nevskiy Prospekt 57.
Tel: 380 2001.
Open: 6.30pm–midnight.
Metro: Mayakovskaya.

Le Français ★★★★
More than 60 traditional
French dishes and a
big choice of French
wines.
Galernaya Ulitsa 20.
Tel: 315 2465.
www.lefrancais.spb.ru.
Open: 11am–1am.
Metro: Sadovaya.

Taleon ★★★★
Exclusive French
restaurant.
Reki Moyki Naberezhnaya
59. Tel: 324 9911.
www.taleon.ru. Open:
7pm–3am. Booking (and

formal dress) essential.
Metro: Nevskiy Prospekt.

MOSCOW BARS AND CAFÉS
Bars
30/7
Expertly concocted
cocktails and a lounge
with great views.
Petrovka 30/7. Tel: 495
650 5951. Open: 24 hours.
Metro: Pushkinskaya.

Bavarius
Beer house serving large
selection of local and
imported beer, and meals
ideally suited to them.
Komsomolskiy Prospekt
21/10. Tel: 499 245 2395.
Open: noon–midnight.
Metro: Frunzenskaya.
Sadovaya-Triumfalnaya
2/30. Tel: 495 699 4211.
Open: daily
noon–midnight. Metro:
Mayakovskaya.

B B King's
Posters of jazz and blues
greats, appropriate live
music, bar food.
Sadovaya-Samotechnaya
Ulitsa 4. Tel: 495 699
8206. Open: noon–
midnight. Metro: Tsvetnoi
Bulvar.

Booze Bub
Watering hole and sports
bar open 24 hours.

Potapovskiy Pereulok 5.
Tel: 495 621 4717.
Metro: Chistye Prudy.

Cafés
Aristokrat
Coffee house in a 19th-century house. Great coffees, teas and cakes.
Myasnitskaya 37.
Tel: 495 924 0702.
Open: 10am–midnight.
Metro: Chistye Prudy.

Bookafe
Refreshingly low-key, modish café with photography and art books to hand.
Sadovaya-Samotechnaya 13. Tel: 495 694 0356.
Open: 11am–2am.
Metro: Tsvetnoi Bulvar.

Café Buloshnaya
Beautifully fashioned 19th-century tea parlour and tranquil escape from Moscow's hurly-burly.
Lyalin Pereulok 7/2.
Tel: 495 917 3295.
Open: 9am–midnight.
Metro: Chkalovskaya.

Coffee Bean
Numerous cafés in the city with excellent coffee.
Pokrovka 18. Tel: 495 623 9793. Open: Mon–Thur 8am–10pm, Fri–Sat 8am–11pm, Sun 9am–10pm.
Metro: Kitay-Gorod.

Tverskaya 10. Tel: 495 788 6357. Open: Mon–Sat 8am–11pm, Sun 9am–11pm.
Metro: Pushkinskaya.

ST PETERSBURG BARS AND CAFÉS
Bars
Dickens
Whether it's pre-club drinks, a full-blown restaurant meal or post-club breakfast you are after, this British pub has it all and much besides.
Reky Fontanky Naberezhnaya 108.
Tel: 310 6388. Open: 8am–2am. Metro: Sennaya.

James Cook
Open later than most, this pub-cum-café is a fine place to round off a night in SPB.
Shvedskiy Pereulok 2.
Tel: 312 3200.
Open: Sun–Thur 9am–2am, Fri 9am–4am, Sat 10am–4am.
Metro: Nevskiy Prospekt.

Liverpool
Blues, jazz and rock every night from 9pm.
Mayakovskovo 16. Tel: 579 2054. Open: noon–1am. Metro: Ploshchad Vosstaniya.

Piyanni Soldat
The 'Drunken Soldier' has one room divided into four levels plied by uniformed waitresses.
Ulitsa Nekrasova 44.
Tel: 579 1789. Open: noon–1am. Metro: Chernyshevskaya.

Cafés
Idealnaya Chashka
A chain of coffee and confectionery cafés.
Sadovaya Ulitsa 25.
Tel: 310 0404.
www.idealcup.ru

Laima Bistro
Excellent Russian bistro chain, serving snacks and light meals. No smoking or credit cards.
Griboyedova Kanala Naberezhnaya 14–16.
Tel: 315 5545.
Open: 24 hours.
Metro: Nevskiy Prospekt/ Gostiny Dvor.

Marrakesh
Slip off your shoes to enjoy herbal teas and North African desserts at this Moroccan tea house.
Karavannaya Ulitsa 3/35.
Tel: 571 8047.
Open: Sun–Thur 1pm–1am, Fri–Sat 1pm–3am.
Metro: Gostiny Dvor/ Nevskiy Prospekt.

Vodka

'Drinking is the joy of Russians,' declared Prince Vladimir in 988. Over a millennium later, Russians are still hard at it.

The national drink is vodka, meaning 'little water', reputedly invented by Russian monks in the 14th century. Produced from filtered water and pure spirit, it is drunk neat, chilled and in one gulp, traditionally followed by a bite of pickled cucumber or a deep sniff from a chunk of black bread – said to help it go down more smoothly.

Peter the Great's troops received two mugfuls daily by Imperial decree. Peter established the state monopoly on vodka production, and used the proceeds to help finance his wars. Vodka played its role in the Great Patriotic War of 1941–5. On 22 August 1941, Stalin issued a decree to ensure 100 grams of vodka were issued daily to all soldiers on the front line. Today, vodka revenues rake in more than income tax.

A 1980 report concluded that drinking had become a threat to national security. Gorbachev cut vodka production drastically in the hope of forcing the population back to the workplace. But the policy succeeded only in driving production underground and emptying shops of sugar, potatoes and eau de cologne, while employees spent ever longer queuing for the few bottles that remained on sale.

Russian vodka is drunk in 'grams', preferably 100 grams at any one time. Foreign visitors who do not wish to drink such a large quantity may only be expected to drink 50 grams! Sipping vodka, or mixing it with any alcohol-free beverage, should be avoided at all costs, but you are allowed to 'wash down' vodka with another beverage after drinking it straight.

Russians do not accept any excuses for not having a *stakan* (glass/shot of vodka) with them. If visitors try to excuse themselves, their hosts usually take it as a joke and pour them a glass anyway! Excuses that tend to work include the need to drive home (make sure you have a car in Moscow) and diabetes, and women are excused by pregnancy, but their partners will be expected to drink even more to celebrate this joyous occasion.

The **Vodka Museum** in Moscow (*open: daily 11am–9pm. Izmailovskoe Shosse, Moscow. Tel: 499 166 5057. www.vodkamuseum.ru*) sheds more light on the Russians' national tipple.

Accommodation

In the days when tourism was a state monopoly, the foreign traveller was lucky to know in which hotel he was to be housed before arrival at the airport. Happily, the situation has changed for the better. Although Russia's hotel industry still has some catching up to do, you can now enjoy first-class standards of accommodation – if you can afford it.

The adventurous might consider staying with a Russian family for an unrivalled insider's view of what life is really like (*see p175*).

The first step

Choose and book accommodation with your travel agent before arrival.

Alternatively, shop around on the internet or contact one of the growing number of accommodation agencies in both cities (*see p189 for a selection of agents*).

Good-quality, Western-style hotels are relatively few in number and often heavily booked. Their ex-Soviet

You can stay in stylish old hotels dating back to the pre-communist era

counterparts are frequently all but empty, yet the barrage of paperwork, calls to the police and hostile reception staff that greet unexpected arrivals are a serious disincentive to fully independent travel. At the very least, book your St Petersburg accommodation while you are in Moscow (and vice versa). (*See p175 for bed and breakfast booking.*)

Selecting a hotel

Neither Moscow nor St Petersburg has the huge number of affordable hotels and guest houses that characterise, say, London or Paris. This simplifies your choice.

Western-run hotels are four or five star, mostly operated by chains such as Radisson or Marco Polo, and are all one would expect from an international luxury hotel, the tariff included. Expect to pay between £140 and £200 for a double room.

Former Soviet establishments are significantly cheaper (the better ones cost about £70 for a double, the less pleasant as little as £15), but are generally spartan, unloved and under-maintained (though renovation at some has improved standards). Their own star grading system is a deceptive guide to the quality within. Broken televisions, eccentric plumbing, drunken trade union delegations and vermin are not considered grounds for a discount. Four stars is the top of the range and the least likely to offer the above inconveniences. However, it is still vital to check in

advance and ask when the establishment was last refurbished.

Location

Most Western-style hotels are situated in the centre of both cities. Those that are not offer a regular shuttle service to and from the centre. Location is more critical with regard to Soviet-style hotels, many of which are in industrialised suburbs: the savings may not be worth the trouble of commuting into town each day. Check the location carefully before booking.

Having chosen the hotel, ask for a room that does not face the street. Russian traffic runs on low-grade petrol – the smell can be overpowering – and at night you run the risk of being kept awake by the noise. In summer mosquitoes can be a problem.

Understanding your hotel

There should be no difficulties with a Western-style hotel. You will find most staff speak English. Restaurants, gymnasiums and souvenir shops are liberally distributed about the premises. Breakfast is usually included in the room price (you generally have the choice from an extensive buffet) and credit cards are accepted. Most will also offer facilities for changing money and many are equipped with state-of-the-art business centres.

Soviet-style establishments, however, work according to their own subculture, which takes some adjusting to. With your key you will be issued a pass essential to getting past the doorman later. Always lock your door and do not open it to unknown visitors under any circumstances. The key should be left with the lady manning your floor, the *dezhurnaya*, who can also serve you tea or at least hot water.

The hotel's restaurants and bars may keep illogical hours – it is worth checking to avoid disappointment later. Breakfast is rarely included in the room price and credit cards are almost never accepted.

Checking out can be a time-consuming process since the *dezhurnaya* will want to inspect your rooms to ensure towels, etc. are all intact. Give yourself ample time if you have a plane or train to catch!

Hostels

A good option for the budget-conscious is a youth hostel, aimed at Western backpackers but clean and secure and an excellent source of camaraderie and local knowledge. Accommodation is generally in dormitories, though some two-bed rooms are available. A communal breakfast is offered in the morning and self-catering facilities are available. There are now many hostels in each of the two cities and booking ahead of a planned trip is essential to avoid disappointment, especially during high points of the season such as the St Petersburg White Nights. Hostel staff speak English and they can also help arrange visa invitations (*see pp178–9*)

The elegant façade of the Ritz Carlton in Moscow

Hotel Metropol in Moscow opened in 1901

and organise travel tickets within Russia – between Moscow and St Petersburg or something as exotic as the Trans-Siberian Railway.

Self-catering

Self-catering accommodation in furnished apartments is not a feasible short-term option, but those who are planning to stay for a month or more should check the English-language press classified sections for rental advertisements. Most flats are very basic by Western standards of comfort. Those with modern electrical appliances and a fresh coat of paint are likely to be as expensive as rented accommodation in any other major capital. However, it works out much cheaper than a hotel.

Bed and breakfast

Living with a Russian family is the ideal way to become acquainted with life beyond the holiday brochures and tour buses. It is also surprisingly well organised in both cities and can be pre-booked prior to arrival.

Prices per night vary but range from about £15 to £20 for rooms checked by agency staff and for a mammoth Russian breakfast. Most of the hosts either speak fluent English or are students keen to improve their grasp of the language. Some may be happy to work as a driver for the duration of your stay or might offer their services as a guide to the city.

For Moscow and St Petersburg, contact **Home Families Association**, *www.hofa.ru*

WHERE TO STAY

The star ratings indicate the average cost of a double room per night:

★ less than 1,000R

★★ 1,000R–2,500R

★★★ 2,500R–5,000R

★★★★ More than 5,000R

Moscow

Godzillas Hostel ★/★★

The capital's best backpacker hostel has comfortable dorms, singles and doubles, as well as a welcoming atmosphere.

Bolshoi Karetniy Pereulok 6. Tel: 495 699 4223.
www.godzillashostel.com.
Metro: Tsvetnoi Bulvar.

Trans-Siberian Hostel ★★

Another great hostel with a very central location and sound facilities, including a kitchen.

Barashevskiy Pereulok 12.
Tel: 495 916 2030.
Metro: Kurskaya/
Kitay-Gorod.

Izmailovo Gamma Delta ★★★

A huge hotel complex 9km (5½ miles) northeast of the city centre with business-standard rooms and a plethora of services.

Izmailovskoe Shosse 71.
Tel: 495 737 7070.

www.izmailovo.ru.
Metro: Partizanskaya.

Warsaw Hotel ★★★

The 140 renovated rooms in this Soviet-era stalwart represent excellent value for money.

Leninskiy Prospekt 2.
Tel: 495 238 7701.
Metro: Oktyabrskaya.

East-West Hotel ★★★/★★★★

Intimate and welcoming 27-room hotel in the city centre. Rooms are well maintained and the staff are friendly.

Tverskoi Bulvar 14.
Tel: 495 232 2857.
www.eastwesthotel.ru.
Metro:
Tverskaya/Okhotny Ryad.

Sovietsky Hotel ★★★/★★★★

5km (3 miles) northwest of Red Square but near the metro, this hotel toys with a lacy 1930s Soviet theme, including lots of Stalinist-era crystal, the odd neoclassical frill and heavy red curtains.

Leningradskiy Prospekt 32/2 Tel: 495 960 2000.
www.sovietsky.ru. Metro:
Dinamo.

Arbat Hotel ★★★★

Not much to look at from the outside, this

Soviet hotel has received a thorough makeover inside. The result is well-appointed rooms that retain a little pre-1991 charm.

Plotnikov Pereulok 12.
Tel: 499 244 7635.
www.president-hotel.net.
Metro: Smolenskaya.

Golden Apple ★★★★

A spick-and-span boutique hotel boasting some unusual room design. Ask to see yours before you commit, as not all will be to everyone's liking.

11 Malaya Dmitrovka.
Tel: 495 980 7000.
www.goldenapple.ru.
Metro: Pushkinskaya.

Hilton Leningradskaya ★★★★

Housed in one of Moscow's Stalinist-era skyscrapers, the Hilton is almost top of the pile and has history to boot. The views across Moscow from some of the rooms are worth the hefty room rates on their own.

Ulitsa Kalanchevskaya 21/40. Tel: 495 627 5550.
Metro: Komsomolskaya.

Metropol ★★★★

Arguably the Russian capital's best place to stay

with luscious art nouveau interiors and a central location just a few minutes' walk from Red Square.
Teatralniy Proezd 1/4. Tel: 499 501 7800. www. metropol-moscow.ru. Metro: Lubyanka.

St Petersburg
Nord Hostel ★/★★
Probably St Petersburg's best backpacker digs situated near the Hermitage.
Bolshaya Morskaya Ulitsa 10. Tel: 571 0342. www.nordhostel.com. Metro: Nevskiy Prospekt.
Hotel Olgino ★/★★★
This motel and campsite, 18km (11 miles) from the city centre, is for those who would like to combine the pleasures of the city with the bracing sea air of the Gulf of Finland.
18 Km Primorskoe Highway E18. Tel: 633 0205. www.hotel-olgino.spb.ru
Azimut Hotel St Petersburg ★★★
Renovation is ongoing at this Soviet-era mega-hotel, but the improved rooms are good value for money. The views across St Petersburg can be incredible.
Lermontovskiy Prospekt 43/1. Tel: 740 2640. www.azimuthotels.ru. Metro: Sennaya/Sadovaya.
Polikoff Hotel ★★★
A cosy mini-hotel with 15 rooms and a guest kitchen. The location cannot be beaten.
Nevskiy Prospekt 64/11. Tel: 995 3488. www.polikoff.ru. Metro: Nevskiy Prospekt.
Repin Hotel ★★★
Another small hotel on Nevskiy Prospekt, this time with Scandinavian-style furnishings.
Nevskiy Prospekt 136. Tel: 950 011 7021 (mobile). www.repin-hotel.ru. Metro: Nevskiy Prospekt.
Antique Hotel Rachmaninov ★★★★
Occupying the former home of composer Rachmaninov, this delightful place has antique touches and a warm, cosy ambience.
Kazanskaya Ulitsa 5. Tel: 571 7618. www. hotelrachmaninov.com. Metro: Nevskiy Prospekt.
Ermitage Hotel ★★★★
A classy establishment just a stone's throw from the real Hermitage. Good service is guaranteed here.
Millionnaya Ulitsa 11. Tel: 571 5497. www.ermitage-hotel.com. Metro: Nevskiy Prospekt.
Grand Hotel Europe ★★★★
The Grand's rooms come with a hefty price tag but are the last word in opulence. Breakfast costs more than some mid-range hotel rooms!
Mikhailovskaya Ulitsa 1/7. Tel: 329 6611. www. grandhoteleurope.com. Metro: Nevskiy Prospekt.
Oktyabrskaya Hotel ★★★★
A mixed bag of sad Soviet and high-ceilinged 19th-century quarters characterise this finely positioned hotel near the Moscow Station – so view before you commit.
Ligovskiy Prospekt 10/118. Tel: 578 1515. Metro: Ploshchad Vosstaniya.
Petro Palace Hotel ★★★★
Another upmarket hotel near the Hermitage, with classical antique touches.
Malaya Morskaya Ulitsa 14. Tel: 571 2880. www. petropalacehotel.com. Metro: Nevskiy Prospekt.

Accommodation

Practical guide

Arriving

By air

Moscow has two international airports. From **Domodedovo** take the shuttle train to Paveletsky Vokzal (station) and then metro (journey time 45 minutes). Tickets are in roubles only. From **Sheremetyevo-2** the quickest option is to take the new Aeroexpress train to Savyolovskiy Vokzal, which runs from 5.30am until midnight. Taking a taxi puts you at great risk of being seriously ripped off to the tune of hundreds of dollars.

For flight information telephone: (Domodedovo) 495 933 6666. *www.domodedovo.ru*; (Sheremetyevo-2) 495 232 6565. *www.sheremetyevo-airport.ru*

St Petersburg's international airport is **Pulkovo 2**. For current information on international flights, call *704 3444. www.pulkovoairport.ru*

The airport is 17km ($10^1/2$ miles) south of the city. Taxis are a slightly cheaper means of travelling in St Petersburg than in Moscow, though it's probably wiser to pre-arrange a transfer through your hotel. The bus No 13 route runs into the city, stopping at Moskovskaya Ploshchad (*metro: Moskovskaya*).

By rail

Those arriving in Moscow by train from Western Europe come into Belorussky Vokzal, served by the metro's circle and green lines. Trains to St Petersburg from Helsinki pull into Finlayndsky Vokzal at Ploshchad Lenina metro, while those from Berlin arrive at Vitebsky Vokzal, Pushkinskaya metro.

Visas and registration

All visitors to Russia need a valid passport with at least one blank page and six months before the expiry date. Visas (obligatory) are obtainable from Russian embassies or consulates. A fee is payable and the process is bureaucratic and time-consuming. Package tourists can expect their tour operator to arrange the relevant tourist visa. To qualify you need proof of pre-booked accommodation for the relevant period. Visitors staying in hostels or homestays should contact a visa agency in their home country well in advance of travelling (*see below*).

Business visas, valid for three, six or twelve months, can be obtained through an official letter from an organisation in Russia, accredited to the Ministry of Foreign Affairs. Holders of business visas do not need proof of pre-booked accommodation. Visitors staying in large hotels will automatically obtain the obligatory visa registration stamp. Those in hostels or homestays should consult the host agency before travelling. If you fail to obtain a registration stamp from the Passport and Visa Directorate (formerly known as OVIR) you will be liable for a hefty fine. Usually your hotel will take care of registration. For information on the latest visa regulations and how to apply, contact your nearest Russian consulate.

The following travel agencies abroad specialise in Russia or in visa applications:

UK:

Alpha-Omega Travel,
16 Eldon Place, Bradford BD1 3AZ.
Tel: 01274 760600.
www.alpha-omega.ru

Real Russia,
3 The Ivories,
Northampton St, London N1 2HY.
Tel: 020 7100 7370.
www.realrussia.co.uk

USA:

Complete Travel & Visa Center,
40 Rector Street, Suite 1504, New York, NY 10006. Tel: 212 233 3332.
Fax: 212 233 0916. www.travelvisas.net

Camping

Moscow has no real campsites to speak of and St Petersburg has very limited options. Very few people consider camping an option in Russia for obvious reasons of personal security.

Children

Children up to seven travel free on public transport. Aeroflot allows one child under five to travel with each accompanying adult on its internal flights. Most of the museums and parks offer discount tickets for children. Disposable nappies and baby foods are on sale in most Western-style supermarkets (*see p143*).

Climate

St Petersburg is slightly warmer than Moscow, but the damp and the Baltic breezes can make it seem colder. March and early April bring slush and puddles during the thaw. Mid-May to mid-September sees temperatures averaging 18°C (64°F) in both cities, often reaching 25–30°C (77–86°F) in July and August. Winter draws in quickly by mid-October.

Conversion tables

Russia uses the same sizes as the rest of Europe for some items of clothing but other items can vary.

Crime

The tourist is unlikely to encounter the much-reported organised criminal activity. Petty theft is comparable to that in major cities elsewhere. Do not leave

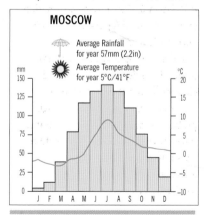

WEATHER CONVERSION CHART

25.4mm = 1 inch
°F = 1.8 × °C + 32

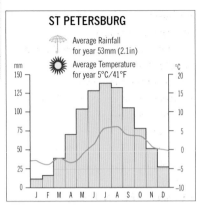

ST PETERSBURG

Average Rainfall
for year 53mm (2.1in)

Average Temperature
for year 5°C/41°F

mm   °C
150   20
125   15
100   10
75   5
50   0
25   -5
0   -10

J F M A M J J A S O N D

valuables unattended, do not carry large amounts of cash, and always lock the door to your hotel room. Be wary if a stranger invites you home. At night, be careful with taxi rides and keep to well-lit streets. Avoid the gangs of gypsy children in areas frequented by foreigners – they strip their victims of valuables like locusts. On overnight trains lock your compartment door and do not open it to strangers.

Customs

Russian customs regulations are many and ever-changing, but real problems only arise if you try to export tradable quantities of commodities like caviar, or antiques. This means steering clear of genuine icons and *objets d'art* (including books) produced more than 20 years ago. Items of military hardware and uniforms are also best avoided. Permits to export are available through the **Office for Culture** (*tel: 495 244 7675*).

Fill in a currency declaration form on arrival and departure, and get receipts for each time you change money.

CONVERSION TABLE

FROM	TO	MULTIPLY BY
Inches	Centimetres	2.54
Feet	Metres	0.3048
Yards	Metres	0.9144
Miles	Kilometres	1.6090
Acres	Hectares	0.4047
Gallons	Litres	4.5460
Ounces	Grams	28.35
Pounds	Grams	453.6
Pounds	Kilograms	0.4536
Tons	Tonnes	1.0160

To convert back, for example from centimetres to inches, divide by the number in the third column.

MEN'S SUITS

UK	36	38	40	42	44	46	48
Rest of Europe	46	48	50	52	54	56	58
USA	36	38	40	42	44	46	48

DRESS SIZES

UK	8	10	12	14	16	18
France	36	38	40	42	44	46
Italy	38	40	42	44	46	48
Rest of Europe	34	36	38	40	42	44
USA	6	8	10	12	14	16

MEN'S SHIRTS

UK	14	14.5	15	15.5	16	16.5	17
Rest of Europe	36	37	38	39/40	41	42	43
USA	14	14.5	15	15.5	16	16.5	17

MEN'S SHOES

UK	7	7.5	8.5	9.5	10.5	11
Rest of Europe	41	42	43	44	45	46
USA	8	8.5	9.5	10.5	11.5	12

WOMEN'S SHOES

UK	4.5	5	5.5	6	6.5	7
Rest of Europe	38	38	39	39	40	41
USA	6	6.5	7	7.5	8	8.5

Driving

Russian driving practices are hair-raising, and travelling by car in Moscow and St Petersburg is not recommended. Roads are potholed and badly signposted, and you are at the mercy of the GAI, the ill-reputed traffic police. Drivers must possess a home and international driving licence with Russian language insert (available from the AA). Russians often drive without insurance, so have a comprehensive policy (if driving a rented car, check the level and conditions of cover). The legal blood alcohol content level is just 0.03 per cent, making it difficult to have even one drink if you intend to drive.

Traffic drives on the right. The speed limit in built-up areas is 60kph (37mph) and 80kph (50mph) on highways. Petrol – *benzin* – comes in several octane grades, 95 being the best for Western cars.

Car hire agencies operating in Moscow and St Petersburg include:
Avis: Moscow, *tel: 495 744 0733. www.avis-moscow.ru*
Biracs: Moscow, *tel: 495 505 2579. www.biracs.ru*
Europcar: International Reservations, *tel: 495 775 7565. www.europcar.com*
Hertz: Moscow, *tel: 495 971 3065.* St Petersburg, *tel: 326 4505. www.hertz.ru*

Electricity

Most of Russia runs on 220V and uses continental European-style 2-pin plugs. Many electrical stores and Western-style supermarkets sell adaptors.

Embassies and consulates

Moscow (embassies)
Australia: *Podkolokolny Pereulok 10a. Tel: 495 956 6070. www.russia.embassy.gov.au*
Canada: *Starokonyushenniy Pereulok 23. Tel: 495 925 6000.*
New Zealand: *Povarskaya 44. Tel: 495 956 3579. www.nzembassy.com*
Republic of Ireland: *Grokholskiy Pereulok 5. Tel: 495 937 5911.*
UK: *Smolenskaya Naberezhnaya 10. Tel: 956 7200. http://ukinrussia.fco.gov.uk*
USA: *Bolshoi Deviatinskiy Pereulok 8. Tel: 495 728 5000. http://moscow.usembassy.gov*

St Petersburg (consulates)
UK: *Ploshchad Proletarskoi Diktatury 5. Tel: 320 3200.*
USA: *Furshtadskaya 15. Tel: 331 2600. www.stpetersburg-usconsulate.ru*

Emergency telephone numbers

The following can be called free of charge in both cities from any public telephone:
Fire *01*
Police *02*
Ambulance *03*

In the event of theft or illness, a better bet is to turn to your hotel or embassy.

Health

Your travel insurance policy should give good cover for medical treatment. Russian hospitals are grim, and foreign-staffed clinics are expensive. Both cities offer well-stocked pharmacies, but travellers are advised to bring their own prescribed medications and contraceptives. No injections are mandatory before arrival, though some doctors advise diphtheria and hepatitis inoculations. AIDS is present, of course.

Moscow's tap water is allegedly safe. In St Petersburg, it is better to buy bottled water.

In an emergency, either speak to your embassy doctor or contact the following medical clinics or pharmacies:

Clinics
American Medical Center
Moscow: *Grokholskiy Pereulok. Tel: 495 933 7700. www.amcenter.ru*
American Medical Clinic
St Petersburg: *Reki Moyki Naberezhnaya 78. Tel: 740 2090. www.amclinic.ru*
European Medical Centre
Moscow: *Spiridonievskiy Pereulok 5. Tel: 495 933 6655. www.emcmos.ru*
St Petersburg: *Suvorovskiy Prospekt 60. Tel: 327 0301. www.euromed.ru*
Mediclub Moscow
Moscow: *Michurinskiy Prospekt 56. Tel: 495 931 5018. www.mediclub.ru*

Dental
Moscow:
European Dental Centre,
1-y Nikoloschepovskiy Pereulok 6. Tel: 495 933 0002. Open: Mon–Fri.

St Petersburg:
Dental Palace, *Bolshoi Prospekt. Tel: 325 7500. www.dentalpalace.ru*

Pharmacies
Moscow:
36.6 Pharmacy, *Pokrovka 1. Tel: 495 923 2258.*
Apteka No 51, *Zamlyanoi Val 42. Tel: 495 916 4268.*
Petrovskaya, *Pharmacy Pokrovka 19. Tel: 495 923 2446.*

St Petersburg:
PetroFarm, *Nevskiy Prospekt 22. Tel: 314 5401. Open: 24 hours. Metro: Nevskiy Prospekt/Gostiny Dvor.*
Pharmacy, *Sadovaya 48. Tel: 310 1053. Open: 24 hours. Metro: Sennaya Ploshchad.*

Before travelling always ensure you have adequate travel insurance.

Maps and additional information
The best and most widely available maps for Moscow and St Petersburg are published by the Austrian cartographers **Freytag & Berndt** (*www.freytagberndt.at*). Moscow has no tourist office to speak of, meaning free maps are a rarity.

An excellent source of information for both cities are the handy (and witty) *In Your Pocket* guides (*www.inyourpocket.com*), which can be picked up for free at hotels, restaurants and other tourist spots, or purchased for a nominal price.

Pre-departure, the websites *www.moscow-taxi.com* and *www.saint-petersburg.com* have a lot of information on their respective cities, although not all of it is accurate or up to date.

Media

Foreign newspapers are on sale in hotels and Western-style supermarkets. Several local English-language newspapers are available free, including *The Moscow Times* and *St Petersburg Times*.

Most hotels are equipped with CNN and satellite broadcasts. The Moscow local TV channel shows BBC news in English at 7.45am weekdays and 7.00am at weekends.

Money matters

One rouble is theoretically divided into 100 kopecks, but in practice the lowest denomination is the one rouble coin.

Do not change money on the streets since both city centres are littered with bureaux de change – *obmyen valyuty* – and private deals remain illegal. Banknotes printed before 1993 are no longer legal tender. Dollars and euros are the easiest to change, but torn or marked bills and pre-1988 dollars are often refused. Bring sterling or US dollar denomination traveller's cheques in small values. Cheques are not as useful as credit and debit cards, however, as these can be used in ATMs, which are located around both cities.

Credit and debit cards are generally accepted in foreign-run shops, hotels, larger restaurants and travel agents. Some banks offer cash advances on Visa and MasterCard. In case of theft, phone

Moscow *495 580 9449 (Amex)*, *495 956 4806 (MasterCard, Visa, Diners Club)*. **American Express** is based in Moscow at *Usacheva 33 (tel: 495 933 8400)* and in St Petersburg in *Malaya Morskaya Ulitsa 23 (tel: 326 4500)*.

Opening hours

Shops are open from Monday to Saturday 9am–6 or 7pm. Larger stores stay open until 8pm, and many of them, including foreign-run supermarkets, trade on Sundays. Many kiosks, especially around railway stations, are open 24 hours a day.

Photography

Military bases and the like remain off limits, and militia officers may object if you point a lens directly at them (if so, take note).

For photographic supplies such as memory cards and film, try **Digitalbraz** (*Chistoprudniy Bulvar 12. Tel: 495 928 6628*) in Moscow and **Yarky Mir** (*Nevskiy Prospekt 6. Tel: 335 5500*) in St Petersburg. If your camera breaks while in Russia, local repair shops can work wonders for just a few roubles.

Places of worship
Moscow:

Catholic Chaplaincy: *Kutuzovskiy Prospekt 7/4. Sat 6pm (English and French), Sun 6pm (English).*
Protestant Chaplaincy: *Voznesenskiy Pereulok 8. Sun 3pm.*
www.moscowprotestantchaplaincy.org
(*Cont. on p186*)

Language

Pronunciation

With a few exceptions, Russian words are pronounced the way they are read. Knowing which syllable to stress, however, takes experience. Just speak slowly and hope for the best.

А/а – ah in 'bar'

Б/б – b

В/в – v

Г/г – g except in words like Островского when it is pronounced as a v

Д/д – d

Е/е – yeh in 'yes'

Ё/ё – yoh in 'yoghurt'

Ж/ж – zh in 'treasure'

З/з – z

И/и – ee in 'Eden'

Й/й – softer than the above, like the y in 'joy'

К/к – k

Л/л – l

М/м – m

Н/н – n

О/о – oh in 'fort' when stressed, otherwise ah in 'bar'

П/п – p

Р/р – r, rolled like an Italian r

С/с – s

Т/т – t

У/у – oo in 'school'

Ф/ф – f

Х/х – kh in the Scottish 'loch'

Ц/ц – ts in 'pretzel'

Ч/ч – ch in 'church'

Ш/ш – sh in 'shoe'

Щ/щ – shch in 'fresh cheese'

Ы/ы – i in 'ilk' but more guttural

Э/э – e in 'end'

Ю/ю – yoo in 'universe'

Я/я – ya in 'yard'

Ь, Ъ – soft sign and hard sign – both affect preceding consonant

Basic words and phrases

yes – da – ДА

no – nyet – НЕТ

please – pazhalsta – ПОЖАЛУЙСТА

thank you – spaseeba – СПАСИБО

excuse me/I'm sorry – izvineetyeh – ИЗВИНИТЕ

good morning – dobroye ootra – ДОБРОЕ УТРО

good afternoon – dobry dyen – ДОБРЫЙ ДЕНЬ

good evening – dobry vyecher – ДОБРЫЙ ВЕЧЕР

good night – spakoiny nochi – СПОКОЙНОЙ НОЧИ

I have ... – oo menya ... – У МЕНЯ...

I haven't ... – oo menya nyet ... – У МЕНЯ НЕТ ...

Do you speak English? – Vwi gavareetyeh pa angleesky? – ВЫ

ГОВОРИТЕ ПО АНГЛИЙСКИЙ?

I do not understand – Yah nye pani*mah*yoo – Я НЕ ПОНИМАЮ

Repeat it, please – Pavta*reet*yeh paz*hal*sta – ПОВТОРИТЕ ПОЖАЛУЙСТА

May I?/Do you mind? – *Mozh*na? – МОЖНО?

How much does … cost? – S*kol*ka stoyit …? – СКОЛЬКО СТОИТ …?

yesterday – vch*erah* – ВЧЕРА

today – *sevod*nyah – СЕГОДНЯ

tomorrow – *zav*tra – ЗАВТРА

at what time …? – vah s*kol*ka …? – ВО СКОЛЬКО …?

where is …? – gdyeh …? – ГДЕ …?

here – zdyes – ЗДЕСЬ

there – tam – ТАМ

near – *bleez*ka – БЛИЗКО

far – dal*ekoh* – ДАЛЕКО

behind – zah – ЗА

opposite – na*protiv* – НАПРОТИВ

in front of – py*ered* – ПЕРЕД

to the right – na*prav*a – НАПРАВО

to the left – na*lyev*a – НАЛЕВО

straight on – vper*yod* – ВПЕРЁД

street – *ool*itsa – УЛИЦА

petrol station – benzaka*lonk*a – БЕНЗОКОЛОНКА

airport – ayero*port* – АЭРОПОРТ

railway station – vokz*al* – ВОКЗАЛ

platform – plat*form*a – ПЛАТФОРМА

bus stop – asta*nov*ka – ОСТАНОВКА

metro station – *stah*ntsia m*etroh* – СТАНЦИЯ МЕТРО

price – ts*ena* – ЦЕНА

ticket office – *ka*ssa – КАССА

ticket – bil*yet* – БИЛЕТ

Quantity

one – a*deen* – ОДИН

two – dva – ДВА

three – tree – ТРИ

four – che*teer*i – ЧЕТЫРЕ

five – pyat – ПЯТЬ

six – shyest – ШЕСТЬ

seven – syem – СЕМЬ

eight – *voh*syem – ВОСЕМЬ

nine – *dyev*yat – ДЕВЯТЬ

10 – *dyes*yat – ДЕСЯТЬ

100 – stoh – СТО

1,000 – *tees*yacha – ТИСЯЧА

a little – nye*mnoh*ga – НЕМНОГО

enough – *khv*ahtit – ХВАТИТ

too many/too much – *sleesh*kom *mnoh*ga – СЛИШКОМ МНОГО

Days

Monday – pani*dyel*nik – ПОНЕДЕЛЬНИК

Tuesday – *vtor*nik – ВТОРНИК

Wednesday – sry*edah* – СРЕДА

Thursday – *chet*vyehrg – ЧЕТВЕРГ

Friday – *pyat*nitsa – ПЯТНИЦА

Saturday – soo*boht*a – СУББОТА

Sunday – voskr*esen*yeh – ВОСКРЕСЕНЬЕ

Mosque: *Vypolzov Pereulok 7.*
Tel: 495 681 4904.
Synagogue: *Arkhipova Ulitsa 14.*
Tel: 495 923 9697.

St Petersburg:

Lutheran Church of St Peter, *Nevskiy Prospekt 22–24. Tel: 312 0798.*
Roman Catholic Church of St Catherine, *Nevskiy Prospekt 32–34. Tel: 311 5795/7170.*
Mosque: *Kronverkskiy Prospekt 7. Tel: 233 9819.*
Synagogue: *Lermontovskiy Prospekt 2 (behind the Mariinskiy Theatre). No phone.*

Post

Stamps, postcards and envelopes can be bought in most hotels, but the Russian postal service is best not relied upon for important letters and packages.

Moscow's Main Post Office is at *Myasnitskaya 26/2. Open: Mon–Fri 8am–8pm, Sat–Sun 9am–7pm*; in St Petersburg, the Main Post Office is at *Pochtamtskaya 9. Open: 24 hours.*

The following international courier agencies operate out of both cities:
DHL *Tel: 495 956 1000* (Moscow). *www.dhl.ru*
Federal Express *Tel: 495 788 8881* (Moscow); *tel: 325 8825* (St Petersburg). *www.fedex.com*
TNT *Tel: 800 2777* (Moscow); *718 3330* (St Petersburg). *www.tnt.com*
UPS *Tel: 495 961 2211* (Moscow). *www.ups.com*

Public transport
Buses, trams and trolleybuses

To make full use of the overground networks requires a high degree of insider knowledge. Tickets valid for all three are sold in strips of ten and can be bought from the drivers. You punch them yourself in the contraptions inside the vehicle (*see also p28*).

Metro

The metro systems are cheap, clean, efficient and safe even at night. A grasp of the Cyrillic alphabet is essential for making sense of the signs.

A neon letter M (red in Moscow, blue in St Petersburg) indicates a station entrance. ВХОД (*vkhod*) on the swing doors means entrance, ВЫХОД (*vykhod*) exit. Tokens (*zhetoni*), or magnetic tickets in Moscow, are on sale at the *kassa* (cash desk), but a modest outlay will buy a monthly season ticket (*prisnoi bilyet*, on sale till the 8th of each month) either for the metro alone (*proezdnoi*) or for overground transport as well (*yedeeni bilyet*). Signs overhead and on the walls indicate the platform.

On arrival, a recorded voice announces the station and the connections. To get out, head for the ВЫХОД В ГОРОД (*vykhod v gorod*) sign. If there is more than one exit, the sign says which takes you where. To change lines, look for ПЕРЕХОД (*perekhod*) – meaning crossing – indicated by a figure walking up steps on a blue background.

The metro in both cities opens before 6am and last changes must be made by 1am in Moscow and 11.30pm in St Petersburg. (See metro maps: Moscow *pp24–5*; St Petersburg *pp28–9*.)

Suburban trains

Many sights outside the city are best reached by the suburban trains, known as *elektrichka*. Tickets, bought at the railway station from the *prigorodny kassi* (often located in a separate part of the station), are very cheap. On the platform, the train will be identified by its final destination, which you should check in the ticket hall. Not every train stops at each station, so check with fellow passengers before boarding.

Taxis

Stopping a taxi (*taksi*) is simple, especially in the centre of town – hold your arm out and a queue of eager drivers will soon pull up. The fare should be agreed before you get in (bear in mind that fares are rapidly approaching world levels). If necessary, write down the fare and the destination.

Many 'taxis' are simply private cars or government vehicles whose drivers are earning a little on the side. They are cheaper, but be very cautious. Never get in a car that already has passengers and do not let the driver pick up additional fares on the way. Women travelling alone at night should avoid taxis completely.

Taxis can be booked from your hotel or call *495 627 0000* (Moscow); *324*

7777 (St Petersburg). Allow at least an hour. Many Western-run hotels have their own taxis, which are far superior to the local service but much pricier.

Travelling between Moscow and St Petersburg

The easiest and cheapest method is by overnight train, leaving either city around midnight and arriving around 8 or 9am. Trains vary in standard with the privately run 'Firmeny' services fastest and most comfortable. Many hotels will arrange your journey for you; independent travellers should go to the station with their passport to buy a ticket in advance. For details and timetables consult the Thomas Cook European Timetable, which is available to buy online at *www.thomascookpublishing.com*, from

A typically ornate corridor at a Moscow Metro station

Thomas Cook branches in the UK or by calling *01733 416477*.

In Moscow, Leningradskiy Vokzal (Leningrad Station) is at *Komsomolskaya Ploshchad 3 (metro: Komsomolskaya)*. In St Petersburg, Moskovskiy Vokzal (Moscow Station) is at *Nevskiy Prospekt 85 (metro: Ploshchad Vosstaniya)*. For timetables log onto *http://eng.rzd.ru* or *www.poezda.net*.

Central Railway Agency Moscow, *Komsomolskaya Ploshchad 5.* *Tel: 495 666 8333.*

Unifest Travel, *tel: 495 234 6555.* Note: *see* **Crime**, *pp179–80*.

Sustainable tourism

Thomas Cook is a strong advocate of ethical and fairly traded tourism and believes that the travel experience should be as good for the places visited as it is for the people who visit them. That's why we firmly support The Travel Foundation: a charity that develops solutions to help improve and protect holiday destinations, their environment, traditions and culture. To find out what you can do to make a positive difference to the places you travel to and the people who live there, please visit *www.thetravelfoundation.org.uk*

Telephones and internet

Public phone boxes taking phone cards have largely replaced the old pay phones using tokens. In Moscow, look out for blue MTTS booths in metro stations and other public places – instructions are available in English at

the press of a button. In St Petersburg, the SPT phone booths are green and white. Phonecards are on sale in metro stations, post offices and some banks and they can also be used for local, intercity and international calls.

For an intercity call on local lines, dial 8 and wait for the tone. The code for Moscow is 495 or 499, for St Petersburg 812. The country code for Russia is 7. To call internationally, dial 8, wait for the tone, dial 10 and the country code: **Australia** *61*, **Canada and USA** *1*, **New Zealand** *64*, **UK** *44*. Then dial the full number.

Many hotels offer Wi-Fi connection, and there are countless hotspots in both cities. Internet cafés are on the wane but you could try **Time Online** (*Okhotny Ryad. Tel: 495 988 6426*) in Moscow or **Café Max** (*Nevskiy Prospekt 90. Tel: 273 6655*) in St Petersburg.

Time

Both cities run three hours ahead of GMT, eight hours ahead of New York time. Summer time, when clocks go forward an hour, begins on the last Saturday of March and ends on the last Saturday of October.

Tipping

With the exception of taxi drivers, who invariably charge double for foreigners, tip as you would anywhere else.

Toilets

Russian public toilets are rare and awful. Carry your own toilet paper and use restaurant or museum facilities when you get the opportunity.

Tourist information

There is no tourist information office to speak of in Moscow so visitors should use the service bureaux in large hotels. St Petersburg is better served. The City Tourist Information Centres are at *Dvortsovaya Ploshchad 12 (Palace Square)* and *Sadovaya 14/52. Tel: 310 8262. www.visit-petersburg.com. Open: Mon–Sat 10am–7pm, Sun (summer only) 10am–6pm*. There's also a branch at the airport (*open: Mon–Fri 10am–7pm*).

Tours in the cities

Patriarshiy Dom (*tel: 495 795 0927*), runs guided tours in English, including a purpose-built Moscow orientation trip. In St Petersburg, ask at the **City Information Centre** (*tel: 310 8262. www.visit-petersburg.com*).

Travel agencies

A number of companies take telephone bookings for internal and international flights. Some book hotels and car hire.
Moscow:
Air Tour, *Leningradskoe Shosse 80, floor 2. Tel: 495 925 3030. www.aerotour.ru*
IntelService Center, *Leninsky Prospekt 29, suites 401–8. Tel: 495 956 4422. www.intelservice.ru*
Intourist, *Prospekt Mira 150. Tel: 495 730 1919.*
Russian Travel Bureau, *Leninsky Prospekt 37. Tel: 495 958 0544.*

Unifest Travel, *Komsomolskiy Prospekt 13. Tel: 495 234 6555.*

St Petersburg:
Cosmos Ltd, *2nd line of Vasilevskiy Island 35. Tel: 327 7256.*
East West Kontaktservice, *Nevskiy Prospekt 105. Tel: 327 3416. www.ostwest.com*
MIR, *Nevskiy Prospekt 11. Tel: 325 7122. www.mirtc.ru*
Russkiye Kruizy, *Nevskiy Prospekt 51. Tel: 325 6120. www.russian-cruises.ru*

Travellers with disabilities

Russia is hard for travellers with disabilities. Access to the metro and other public transport is all but ruled out, and few buildings have ramps.
Access Travel, *6 The Hillock, Astley, Lancs M29 7GW. Tel: 01942 888844. www.access-travel.co.uk*
Mobility International (*www.miusa.org*) may be able to assist with enquiries.
Society for Accessible Travel & Hospitality (SATH), *347 5th Avenue, New York, NY 10016. Tel: 212 447 7284. www.sath.org*

Women travellers

Western-type supermarkets and pharmacies stock sanitary products.

Russian men may seem chauvinistic but do not intend to offend. However, if you feel sexually harassed, cause a public scene rather than ignore it. At night, keep off backstreets and avoid lone taxi rides.

Index

Acknowledgements

Thomas Cook Publishing wishes to thank the photographers, picture libraries and other organisations, to whom the copyright belongs, for the photographs in this book.

DEMETRIO CARRASCO 4, 17a, 17b, 20, 21, 22, 32, 49, 64, 68, 75, 81, 88, 91, 94, 101, 102, 107, 110, 111, 114, 117, 120, 122, 129, 133, 137b, 138, 139a, 139b, 155, 168
DREAMSTIME Dkorolov 1; Webmaxie 7; Rjmiguel 37; Yulia 39; Walrusmail 50; Shipov 84; Optimer 90; Ifphoto 128; Theosid 135; Simfan 136; Onlyreflection 162
FLICKR svonog 9; K R Hamm 23, 159; Skeptically 30, 148; adambrunner 74; Lyalka 82; seriykotik 1970 134; nausicaa 162; Malinki 157; liilliil 175
FOTOLIA Yury Maryunin 63; David Harding 141
JON ARNOLD 14, 15, 35, 45, 48, 57, 66
JON SMITH 62, 144, 145, 163, 174
KEN PATERSON 5, 19, 38, 56, 172
MARC DI DUCA 26, 27, 33, 40, 43, 46, 51, 59, 77, 78, 96, 97, 121, 187
PICTURES COLOUR LIBRARY Albert B Knapp 69; Picture Finders 108
WIKIMEDIA COMMONS Yuriybrisk 55; http://fotocomp.chat.ru 80; Doomych 83; Geevee 116; A A Pasetti 124; Heidas 125
WORLD PICTURES/PHOTOSHOT 118, 137a, 153

For CAMBRIDGE PUBLISHING MANAGEMENT LTD:
Project editor: Frances Darby
Proofreader and indexer: Karolin Thomas
Typesetter: Trevor Double

SEND YOUR THOUGHTS TO
BOOKS@THOMASCOOK.COM

We're committed to providing the very best up-to-date information in our travel guides and constantly strive to make them as useful as they can be. You can help us to improve future editions by letting us have your feedback. If you've made a wonderful discovery on your travels that we don't already feature, if you'd like to inform us about recent changes to anything that we do include, or if you simply want to let us know your thoughts about this guidebook and how we can make it even better – we'd love to hear from you.

Send us ideas, discoveries and recommendations today and then look out for your valuable input in the next edition of this title.

Emails to the above address, or letters to travellers guide Series Editor, Thomas Cook Publishing, PO Box 227, Coningsby Road, Peterborough PE3 8SB, UK.

Please don't forget to let us know which title your feedback refers to!